Psychiatric Slavery

Other titles in the Paperback Library of Thomas Szasz

Anti-Freud: Karl Kraus's Criticism of Psychoanalysis and Psychiatry

Cruel Compassion: Psychiatric Control of Society's Unwanted

The Ethics of Psychoanalysis

Ideology and Insanity: Essays on the Psychiatric Dehumanization of Man

Insanity: The Idea and Its Consequences

Law, Liberty, and Psychiatry

The Manufacture of Madness: A Comparative Study of the Inquisition and the Mental Health Movement

The Myth of Psychotherapy: Mental Healing as Religion, Rhetoric, and Repression

Our Right to Drugs: The Case for a Free Market

Pain and Pleasure: A Study of Bodily Feelings

Psychiatric Justice

Schizophrenia: The Sacred Symbol of Psychiatry

Sex by Prescription: The Startling Truth about Today's Sex Therapy

The Theology of Medicine: The Political-Philosophical Foundations of Medical Ethics

Psychiatric Slavery

Thomas Szasz

With a New Preface by the Author

SYRACUSE UNIVERSITY PRESS

Copyright © 1977 by Thomas S. Szasz
Preface copyright © 1998 by Thomas S. Szasz

All Rights Reserved

First Syracuse University Press Edition 1998
98 99 00 01 02 03   6 5 4 3 2 1

Originally published in 1977 by The Free Press, a division of
Macmillan Publishing Co., Inc.

Library of Congress Cataloging-in-Publication Data

Szasz, Thomas Stephen, 1920–
        Psychiatric slavery / Thomas Szasz ; with a new preface by the
author.
            p.   cm.
        Originally published: New York : Free Press, c1977.
        Includes index.
        ISBN 0-8156-0511-0 (pbk. : alk. paper)
            1. Donaldson, Kenneth—Trials, litigation, etc.   2. Insane—
Commitment and detention—United States.   3. Insanity—
Jurisprudence—United States.   I. Title.
        KF228.D65S93   1998
        362.2'1'092—dc21   97-39251

Manufactured in the United States of America

For

Ursula and George

Contents

	Preface	ix
	Preface to the Original Edition	xxiii
	Acknowledgments	xxvii
1	Justifying the Unjustifiable	1
2	The Case of Kenneth Donaldson	13
3	The Brief for Donaldson	34
4	The Brief for O'Connor	59
5	The Brief for the American Psychiatric Association	66
6	The Supreme Court's Decison in *O'Connor v. Donaldson*	76
7	Interpretations of the Supreme Court's *Donaldson* Decision	89
8	A Right to Treatment or a Right to Treat?	109
9	Chattel Slavery and Psychiatric Slavery	133
	Notes	140
	Index	155

Preface

To commit violent and unjust acts, it is not enough for a government to have the will or even the power; the habits, ideas, and passions of the time must lend themselves to their committal.

—Alexis de Tocqueville [1]

I

When Tocqueville spoke of "unjust acts," he was speaking as a detached observer, viewing state-sanctioned violence as an outsider. From the insider's point of view, state-sanctioned violence is, by definition, just. Prior to the passage of the Thirteenth Amendment, the Constitution of the United States condoned chattel slavery as just and humane. Today, people throughout the civilized world condone psychiatric slavery as just and humane.

Why do I use the phrase *psychiatric slavery* as the title? I admit that its shock value was an attraction. However, my main reason for choosing this title was that I considered the comparison between involuntary servitude and involuntary psychiatry enlightening and valid.*

What is slavery? *Webster's Third Unabridged* defines it as "control by imposed authority" and illustrates its use by citing Jonathan Swift's statement: "All government without the consent of the governed is slavery." As times change, the meanings of words change. Today, the connotations of the term "slavery" are altogether negative. This was not true in ancient societies. There is no condemnation of slavery in the Old or New Testaments or in the Koran. Jews, Christians, and Mohammedans alike owned and traded slaves. And so did Blacks as well as Whites.[2]

These are familiar facts. I mention them to underscore that, throughout most of history, people viewed slavery as a socially indispensable institution and that this perception was shared by masters and slaves alike. In *Psychiatric Slavery* I show how the premise that psychiatric slavery is a socially indispensable institution undergirds all efforts at so-called psychiatric reform and that (with few exceptions) this perception is shared by mental health professionals and mental patients alike.

Since liberty implies responsibility, it is easy to see the source of slavery's appeal: it promises relief from responsibility. Conservatives and libertarians know this well, yet rarely apply it to psychiatry. In 1950, Dean Russell, a respected conservative commentator, wrote:

> Many present-day Americans are trying to avoid this personal responsibility that *is* freedom. They are

---

* This comparison resembles the comparison between the Inquisition and involuntary psychiatry in *The Manufacture of Madness*, subtitled: "A Comparative Study of the Inquisition and the Mental Health Movement."

voting for men who promise to install a system of compulsory, government-guaranteed "security"—a partial return to the slave laws of Georgia that guaranteed all slaves "the right to food and raiment, to kind attention when sick, to maintenance in old age . . ." Just as the law once guaranteed "adequate" medical care for American slaves, so a law to guarantee medical care for all Americans is being demanded today. And who will determine what is adequate medical care for a person?[3]

In a few short years, the sort of health care system Russell warned against has become a part of the "American Way of Life." How could Russell have so underestimated the American people's susceptibility to the siren song of security from life-as-illness? In part, by ignoring psychiatric slavery. Commenting on the government's efforts to protect people from themselves, he declared: "Since they [the Founders] recognized the absurdity of passing laws to protect a person from himself, they left all citizens free to make their own decisions concerning their own personal welfare."[4] Russell could not have been unaware that "mental patients"—cast in that role by others or themselves—were deprived of the right and freed of the duty to "make their own decisions concerning their own personal welfare."

II

Psychiatric slavery—that is, confining individuals in madhouses—began in the seventeenth century, grew in the eighteenth, and became an accepted social custom in the nineteenth century. Because the practice entails depriving individuals innocent of lawbreaking of liberty, it requires appropriate moral and legal justification. The history of psychiatry—especially in its relation to law—is largely the story of changing justifications for psychiatric incarceration. The metamorphosis of one criterion for commitment into another is typically called "psychiatric reform." It is nothing of the kind. The bottom line of the psychiatric balance sheet is fixed: Individuals deemed insane are incarcerated because they are "mentally ill and dangerous to themselves and/or others."* For more than forty years, I have maintained that psychiatric reforms are exercises in prettifying plantations. Slavery cannot be reformed, it can only be abolished. So long as the idea of mental illness imparts legitimacy to the exercise of psychiatric power, psychiatric slavery cannot be abolished.

Power is the ability to compel obedience. Its sources are force from above, and dependency from below. By force I mean the legal and/or physical ability to deprive another person of life, liberty, or property. By dependency I mean the desire or need for others as protectors or providers.** "Nature," observed Samuel Johnson, "has given women so much power that the law has very wisely given them little."[5] The sexual power (domination) women wield (over men who desire them) is here cleverly contrasted with their legal powerlessness (a subservience imposed on them by men).

To distinguish between coercive and non-coercive

---

* In this essay, I limit myself to a critique of the civil commitment of persons not charged with crimes. I consider the insanity defense and other (ab)uses of coercive psychiatry in several of my other books, especially *Law, Liberty, and Psychiatry; Psychiatric Justice;* and *Insanity: The Idea and Its Consequences.*

** The spheres of legitimacy for power and dependency, respectively, are defined by law, custom, and tradition.

means of securing obedience, we must distinguish between force and persuasion, violence and authority. Alfred North Whitehead put it thus: "[T]he intercourse between individuals and between social groups takes one of these two forms, force and persuasion. Commerce is the great example of intercourse by way of persuasion. War, slavery, and governmental compulsion exemplify the reign of force."[6] When Voltaire exclaimed, *"Ecrazez l'infame!"* he was using the word *l'infame* to refer to the power of the Church to torture and kill, not to its power to misinform or mislead.

The potency of power as force, symbolized by the gun, rests on the ability to injure or kill the Other; whereas the potency of power as influence rests on the ability to gratify the Other's desires. The individual who depends on another person for the satisfaction of his needs—or whose needs/desires can be aroused by another—experiences the Other as having power over him. Such is the power of the mother over her infant, of the doctor over his patient, of Circe over Ulysses. In proportion as we master or surmount our desires, we liberate ourselves from this source of domination.

The main source of psychiatric power is coercive domination, exemplified by the imposition of an ostensibly diagnostic or therapeutic intervention on a subject against his will. Its other source is dependency, exemplified by individuals defining themselves as unable to control their own behavior and seeking psychiatric controls. Involuntary psychiatric interventions rest on force, voluntary psychiatric relations on dependency. Equating them is as absurd as equating rape with consensual sex.[*][7]

---

* Some psychiatric critics—opposing the use of psychiatric drugs, electric shock treatment, or psychotherapy—advocate the legal prohibition of one or another method or relationship, on the ground that people need the protection of the state from the "exploitation" intrinsic

When a person suffers—from disease, oppression, or want—he naturally seeks the assistance of persons who have the knowledge, skill, or power to help him or on whom he projects such attributes. In ancient times, priests —believed to possess the ability to intercede with gods— were the premier holders of power. For a long time, curing souls, healing bodies, and relieving social-economic difficulties were all regarded as priestly roles, utilizing both coercive and cooperative interventions. Only in the last few centuries have the roles of priest, physician, and politician become differentiated, as Religion, Medicine, and Politics—each institution allotted its "proper" sphere of influence, each struggling to enlarge its scope and power over the others. Moreover, only in the West has the power of the priest been reduced to the same level as the power of the people, that is, to the opportunity to persuade willing listeners.

The separation of Church and State—that is, withdrawing from religious authorities and organizations the legal authority to use force and denying them funds extracted by force (taxes)*—represents a sharp break in the history of mankind. Although paying lip service to an Almighty, the American Constitution is, in effect, a declaration of the principle that only agents of the state can exercise power legitimately, and that the sole source of the govern-

---

to the practices of psychiatrists and psychotherapists. However, coercive protection from psychiatric treatment is just as patronizing and inimical to dignity-and-liberty as coercive protection from psychiatric illness.

* Many Americans erroneously believe that this condition obtains in all modern democracies. In Britain, there is no formal separation of church and state. In Germany and Switzerland, religious bodies receive moneys collected by the state.

ment's legitimacy is the "happiness of the people," insured by securing "the consent of the governed." Gradually, other western states have adopted this outlook. The Argentinean poet and novelist Adolfo Bioy Casares satirized the resulting "happiness" thus:

> Well then, maybe it would be worth mentioning the three periods of history. When man believed that happiness was dependent upon God, he killed for religious reasons. When man believed that happiness was dependent upon the form of government, he killed for political reasons. After dreams that were too long, true nightmares . . . we arrived at the present period of history. Man woke up, discovered that which he always knew, that happiness is dependent upon health, and began to kill for therapeutic reasons.[8]

Among these therapeutic reasons, the treatment of mental illness occupies a unique place.

III

Who was Kenneth Donaldson and how did he become entangled with the psychiatric system? Briefly, he was an unemployed and unwanted guest in his father's house. When Donaldson refused to remove himself, his father turned to the psychiatric system to remove him. Thus did Kenneth Donaldson become a "guest" of the psychiatric hospital system, officially called a "patient." Ensconced in his new home, Donaldson refused "treatment": He insisted that he was not mentally ill and claimed he was a Christian Scientist. Notwithstanding the internally contra-

dictory character of Donaldson's subsequent complaint—
that his psychiatrists failed to treat his illness—the Supreme Court accepted the case, presumably as an opportunity to reinforce the legitimacy of psychiatric slavery. To
be sure, the "complaint" was not really Donaldson's: The
real protagonists were his handlers, self-anointed reformers of mental health policy, who fabricated an absurdly
hypocritical strategy to advance their own misguided
agenda. Donaldson was merely their foil.

Why did the Donaldson case arouse so much professional and popular interest? Partly because it reopened—
in the context of the new psychopharmacological treatment of mental illness—the question of what constitutes
proper ground for civil commitment; and partly because
Donaldson's malpractice suit reached the Supreme Court.
Today, the case is an arcanum in the history of psychiatric
reform. The issues it raised are, however, of continuing
interest and importance.

Although the long-term confinement of mental patients
in buildings called "mental hospitals"—as Donaldson had
been confined—is no longer fashionable, this does not
mean that the uses of coercive psychiatry have diminished.
On the contrary. While most mental patients are now
housed in buildings *not* called "hospitals," they are still
deprived of liberty, typically by court-ordered "outpatient
commitment" and "drug treatment," euphemisms that disguise their true status more effectively than ever.[9] Since
the Donaldson ruling, psychiatrists routinely invoke claims
such as that patients' "rejection of treatment is itself a
symptom of their illness";[10] that the "cause [of the 'revolving door syndrome'] may be the result of efforts to protect
patients' civil rights—sometimes at the cost of their 'treatment rights' ";[11] and that a "180-day outpatient commit-

ment" policy should be widely adopted because a person who "is suffering from a severe mental disorder . . . lacks the capacity to make an informed decision concerning his need for treatment."[12]

IV

In the modern West, slavery qua slavery is of course as dead as the proverbial dodo. Reviewing a book about Jefferson, Brent Staples declares: "Slavery and the Declaration of Independence can in no way be reconciled. . . . The natural rights section of the Declaration—the most famous words in American history—reflected the belief that personal freedom was guaranteed by God Himself."[13]

Alas, if only it were that simple. The words "freedom-slavery," like the words "right-wrong," are by definition antithetical. Hence, asserting that they cannot be reconciled is a pleonasm. But it is a pleonasm only in principle. In practice it is a temptation—a challenge to people's ingenuity to reconcile irreconcilables—to which many yearn to yield. All that is needed to accomplish the task is hypocrisy and demagoguery: Would-be dominators can then "discover" that the persons they seek to enslave are child-like, the victims of one or another calamity from which they need to be protected. This formula explains why chattel slavery and the Declaration of Independence could coexist for nearly a century; why racial and gender slavery and the Declaration of Independence could coexist well into the twentieth century; and why psychiatric slavery and the Declaration of Independence can now coexist in perfect harmony.

Although modern governments repudiate slavery as the grossest violation of "universal human rights," they continue to exert far-reaching controls over personal conduct, typically justifying coercive paternalism as the *protection of victims from themselves*. Today, the mental patient does not lose his liberty because the state deprives him of it; he loses it because the state declares him to be the beneficiary of a new "constitutional right." In the Donaldson case, the justices of the Supreme Court discovered such a new right, heretofore hidden in the Constitution. They declared: "[A] State cannot constitutionally confine [in a mental hospital] *without more* a nondangerous individual . . ."[14] Psychiatrists lost no time dubbing this "[something] more" the "mental patient's right to treatment." It is important to emphasize that the "treatment" the court had in mind was, by definition, involuntary: It applied *only* to *involuntary mental patients*.

The importance of the Donaldson ruling lay in the fact that it ratified psychiatry's latest medical and therapeutic pretensions. By recognizing the administration of psychoactive drugs to mental patients as bona fide medical treatment, the Supreme Court once again lent the weight of its authority to literalizing the metaphors of mental illness and mental treatment. In addition, by defining involuntary psychiatric interventions—epitomized by involuntary drugging—as bona fide medical treatments, the court redefined involuntary psychiatric interventions from serving the needs of the public to serving the needs of the denominated patient.

The catastrophic implications of these ideas have not yet begun to dawn on American lawmakers, much less on the American people. The "new Nero," C. S. Lewis warned, "will approach us with the silky manners of a doctor."[15] Today, almost a quarter of a century after the Donaldson decision, the Supreme Court is considering whether a terminally ill patient has a constitutional right to physician-assisted suicide. Never mind that the term "terminally ill" is dangerously elastic; that suicide is illegal, prohibited by the *mental health law* of every one of the fifty states; or that because suicide is illegal, it cannot be "assisted," it can only be "accompliced." These are but minor roadblocks retarding our triumphant march toward the full realization of the Therapeutic State. "Even if the treatment is painful, even if it is life-long, even if it is fatal, that"—mocked Lewis—"will be only a regrettable accident; the intention was purely therapeutic."[16]

V

Psychiatric slavery rests on civil commitment and the insanity defense. Each intervention is a paradigm of the perversion of power. If the person called "patient" breaks no law, he has a right to liberty. And if he breaks the law, he ought to be adjudicated and punished in the criminal justice system. It is as simple as that. Nevertheless, so long as conventional wisdom decrees that the mental patient must be protected from himself, that society must be protected from the mental patient, and that both tasks rightfully belong to a psychiatry wielding powers appropriate to the performance of these duties, psychiatric power will remain unreformable.

Some people do threaten society: they commit crimes —that is, acts that deprive others of life, liberty, or property. Society needs protection from such aggressors. What does psychiatry contribute to their management? Civil commitment, inculpating the innocent, and the insanity defense, exculpating the guilty. Both interventions authenticate as "real" the socially useful fictions of mental illness and psychiatric expertise. Both create and confirm the illusion that we are coping wisely and well with vexing social problems, when in fact we are obfuscating and aggravating them. Psychiatric power thus corrupts not only the psychiatrists who wield it and the patients who are subjected to it, but the community that supports it as well.

As Orwell's nightmarish vision of *Nineteen Eighty-Four* nears its climax, O'Brien explains the functional anatomy of power to Winston thus:

[N]o one seizes power with the intention of relinquishing it. Power is not a means; it is an end. One does not establish a dictatorship in order to safeguard a revolution; one makes the revolution in order to establish the dictatorship. The object of persecution is persecution. The object of torture is torture. The object of power is power. Now do you begin to understand me?[17]

The empire of psychiatric slavery is more than three hundred years old and grows daily more all-encompassing. But we have not yet begun to acknowledge its existence, much less to understand its role in our society.

Notes

1. Tocqueville, A. de, quoted in, Auden, W. H. and Kronenberger, L., eds., *The Viking Book of Aphorisms: A Personal Selection* (New York: Dorset Press, 1981), p. 297.

2. Davis, D. B., *The Problem of Slavery in Western Culture* (Ithaca, NY: Cornell University Press, 1966).

3. Russell, Dean, Wards of the government (1950), *Freedom Daily*, 8: 35–43 (January) 1997, pp. 35, 38.

4. *Ibid.,* p. 39.

5. Johnson, S., quoted in, Auden, W. H. and Kronenberger, L., eds., *The Viking Book of Aphorisms: A Personal Selection* (New York: Dorset Press, 1981), p. 172.

6. Whitehead, A. N., *Adventures of Ideas* [1933] (New York: Free Press, 1961), p. 83.

7. Szasz, T. S., "The psychiatric will," *American Psychologist,* 37: 762–770 (July), 1982.

8. Bioy Casares, A., "Plans for an escape to Carmelo," *New York Review of Books,* April 10, 1986, p. 7.

9. See Szasz, Thomas, *Cruel Compassion: Psychiatric Control of Society's Unwanted* (New York: Wiley, 1994).

10. Commitment legislation may emphasize patient rights at expense of treatment, *Clinical Psychiatry News,* 6: 2 (November), 1978.

11. Rubinstein, Jon, The revolving door syndrome pits civil rights against treatment 'rights,' *Legal Aspects of Medical Practice,* 6: 47–49 (May), 1978.

12. Outpatient commitment works, deserves funding, APA testifies, *Psychiatric News,* 3: 4 (September 1), 1995.

13. Staples, Brent, "The Master of Monticello," *New York Times Book Review,* March 23, 1997, p. 7.

14. This volume, p. 79, emphasis added.

15. Lewis, C. S., "The Humanitarian Theory of Punishment," *Res Judicatae* (Melbourne University, Melbourne, Australia), 6: 229, 1953; quoted in, Szasz, T. S., *The Theology of Medicine: The Political-Philosophical Foundations of Medical Ethics* (Syracuse: Syracuse University Press, 1988), p. 130.

16. *Ibid.*

17. Orwell, G., *Nineteen Eighty-Four* (New York: Harcourt Brace, 1949), p. 266.

Preface to the Original Edition

There is, as Richard Weaver has so well put it, no life without prejudice; hence, there is also no person without prejudice.[1] I therefore hasten to acknowledge that the observations and remarks I plan to present are animated and informed by one of my prejudices: namely, that to be a fully human person one must be free and responsible, and must treat others—so far as it is at all possible to do so—as free and responsible persons. This prejudice is diametrically opposed to, and is hence incompatible with, the prejudice that animates and informs institutional psychiatry and those who defend or support its principles and practices.

The judicial branch of the American government, with the Supreme Court at its head, has so far defended and supported involuntary psychiatry. With respect to psychiatry, I therefore find myself squarely in opposition to these authorities. Nevertheless, I have learned from them; and, in my more optimistic moments, I like to believe that they have learned from me and may yet learn more. That, indeed, is one of the good things about "enemies," especially non-violent, respectful, and intelligent enemies. They tell you what you do wrong—which your friends rarely do.

It seems to me that the United States Supreme Court, especially in relation to its struggles with the problem of involuntary psychiatry, has had too many friends and too few enemies. In nearly every case concerning matters of psychiatry that has come before this Court in recent years, virtually every group representing care and compassion, power and prestige, wealth and wisdom, has petitioned the Court as *amicus curiae*.* Since many of the friends of the Court are actually promoting their own self-interests concealed as some individual's or group's constitutional rights, I want to nominate myself, at least for the present occasion, as an enemy, in the sense of opponent, of the Court; and I want to offer my remarks as

* The following are some of the groups and organizations that have submitted *amicus curiae* briefs to the Supreme Court in support of the "right to treatment" for involuntary mental patients: American Association of Mental Deficiency; American Federation of State, County, and Municipal Employees A.F.L.–C.I.O.; American Orthopsychiatric Association; American Psychological Association; American Psychiatric Association; Joseph P. Kennedy Foundation; National Association for Mental Health; National Association for Retarded Citizens; National Center for Law and the Handicapped; National Association for Autistic Children; State of Texas; State of Ohio; State of New Jersey; the federal government.[2]

an *inimicus curiae* brief to that august body. If a clear view of the problems of involuntary psychiatry requires, as I believe it does, emancipation from customary forms of legal and psychiatric thinking about them, then perhaps such a view might be facilitated by a fresh format which departs from the customary friend-of-the-court courtesies, and calls a spade not an agricultural instrument for soil penetration, but a spade.

Acknowledgments

On February 18, 19, and 20, 1976, I enjoyed the privilege of delivering the annual Robert S. Marx Lectures at the University of Cincinnati College of Law. This book is based on, and is a considerably expanded version of, the lectures I presented on that occasion. I should like to take this opportunity to thank, once more, the Robert S. Marx Trustees and the faculty of the University of Cincinnati College of Law for inviting me to be the Marx Lecturer for the academic year 1975–1976.

I wish to thank also Professor Travis Lewin of the Syracuse University College of Law for his generous help in the preparation of this book; Mr. Bruce Ennis for providing me with copies of the briefs for Donaldson and O'Connor; and my daughter, Susan Marie Szasz, for her careful reading of the manuscript and her suggestions for improving it.

To question the ethical basis of slavery, even when the institution was disappearing from view, would be to question fundamental conceptions of God's purpose and man's history and destiny. If slavery were an evil and performed no divinely appointed function, then why had God authorized it in Scripture and permitted it to exist in nearly every nation.[1]

—D. B. Davis, *The Problems of Slavery in Western Culture*

If it was a crime, as many writers asserted, to deprive Americans of their natural liberty, it was actually an act of liberation to remove Negroes from their harsh world of sin and dark superstition. . . . "Though the odious Appellation of Slaves *is annexed to this Trade," wrote a leading economist, ". . . they are certainly treated with great Lenity and Humanity: . . . I cannot but think their condition is much bettered to what it was in their own Country."*[2]

—D. B. Davis, *The Problems of Slavery in Western Culture*

One must remember that slavery was a system, not an individual relationship. No matter how Christian, benevolent, or kind a slaveholder might be, he himself was a captive of the system.[3]

—D. L. Dumond, *Antislavery: The Crusade for Freedom*

I

Justifying the Unjustifiable

I

Before addressing myself to my specific subject—that is, to an analysis of the *Donaldson* case and its implications—I want to offer some brief remarks about two issues whose clarification is crucial to a sensible discussion of any problem of psychiatry and law. They are: first, the distinction between an explanation and a justification; and second, the sorts of justifications human beings have traditionally used to legitimize certain kinds of con-

1

duct on the parts of some persons toward certain others.

Typically, an explanation refers to an event, whereas a justification refers to an act. The difference between these terms is much the same as that between things and persons.

For example, we might ask, "How did lightning kill Jones?" We might then be told that it did so by causing him to have ventricular fibrillation and cerebral anoxia.

We might also ask, "Why did lightning kill Jones?" We might then be told that it was because he continued to play golf during a thunderstorm instead of going back to the clubhouse for a drink, as did his friend Smith. It is important to keep in mind that this sort of statement is an assertion about Jones, the victim, not about lightning or some other aspect of the "cause" of his death.

Our question about why lightning killed Jones may, however, elicit another type of reply, and it is essential that we consider it also. If our interlocutor is a devoutly religious person, or a very mystical one, he might tell us that lightning killed Jones because it was "God's will" (or something of that sort).What is important about this answer is that is purports to explain an event by assimilating it to the model we use for justifying an action. By imagining God as some sort of superman, we picture death caused by lightning as God taking a life. This sort of account pleases and satisfies many people because it fulfills the deeply felt human need for legitimizing, or illegitimizing, not only those things that people do to one another but also those that happen to them.

Suppose, however, that Jones was killed not by lightning but by Smith. We might then reasonably ask both how and why Smith acted as he did. The "how" question seeks to elicit an explanation of Smith's method for causing Jones' death—for example, did he shoot him, poison him, or stab him? What, then, does the "why" question seek? The usual answer is that it seeks an account of Smith's motives or reasons for killing Jones. But this, as I shall now show, is only partly true. Actually, in asking this sort of question about Smith, people usually want to know several things, among which the most obvious and important are: first, Smith's avowed aim or reason for his act; second, his real reason; third, the authorities' official account of the reason; fourth, the psychiatrist's expert opinion about the reason; fifth, the defense attorney's claim about the reason; and sixth, the jury's judgment about the reason.

Each of the above reasons is, strictly speaking, a claim or a conjecture; none is an explanation or a cause, in the sense in which these latter terms are understood and used in natural science. Nevertheless, when confronted with this sort of situation, most people feel, as if it were instinctively, that one or another of the reasons listed is true, and that the others are false. In fact, they may all be true, in the sense that each represents the sincere conviction of the speaker; or they may all be false, in the sense that Smith acted for reasons, perhaps known only to himself, other than any of those articulated in the several conjectures. Let me illustrate this with a simple example.

Suppose that a person, observing patrons ordering food in a restaurant, is asked why one of the customers, named Smith, ordered hamburger rather than lobster. The observer would, of course, first ask Smith, who might explain that he did so because he prefers hamburger to lobster. The observer himself might conjecture that it was because hamburger is cheaper. Who really knows why Smith chose as he did? In the sense in which we can know the chemical composition of hamburger or lobster, no one can know why anyone orders one or the other. The only honest answer to this sort of "why" question is to give an account of the reason for the act *as* claim or conjecture, and to acknowledge frankly the *identity of the claimant or conjecturer.*

Much of the tradition and practice of Anglo-American law is premised on precisely this understanding of human acts and the problems posed by efforts to resolve conflicting claims between persons sensibly and fairly. In both civil and criminal suits, the arbiters assume that plaintiff and defendant, prosecuting attorney and defense attorney, each presents different claims and conjectures about why the protagonists in the judicial drama acted as they did. It is then up to the jury to develop its own conjecture, whose practical implication the court then imposes on the litigants. The jury, or court, does so not because it is necessarily more intelligent or more honest than the participants in the litigation, but because it is more neutral and has the authority and the power to do so.

Psychiatric testimony distorts this model of contesting claimants seeking to convince a presumably impartial jury or court, because insofar as the psychiatrist testifies about why a person acted as he did, he offers a conjecture that he defines and that is widely accepted as a cause. This is epitomized by the belief—now authoritatively accepted as scientifically correct—that some people kill because they hate their victims, others because they want their money, and still others because they have schizophrenia. Mental illness as a cause, and murder as a product of it, must thus be seen for what it is: not simply a mistaken idea, but the manifestation of the judicial acceptance of psychiatrists as scientists of the mind.[2] It is precisely this premise that I have attacked in my past analyses of legal psychiatry, and that I want to single out

4

here as a preliminary test of our critical spirit. Either we accept this psychiatric idolatry—in which case we regard the principles and practices of modern forensic psychiatry as progressive and scientific, or we reject it—in which case we regard psychiatric pronouncements on the human mind, especially when offered in courts of law, as agnostics regard theological pronouncements on God.

II

Let us now consider how we justify human actions. My initial proposition in this connection is that the most powerful justification for an act, and especially for a socially established practice, is no justification at all. The most completely justified forms of conduct are those for which no justification is offered because none is expected.

A dramatic example of this is the absence of any reference to slavery in the Constitution of the United States of America.* Another is the absence, until recently, of any reference in psychiatric texts to the fact that many so-called psychiatric patients are, in fact, patients against their will. Not mentioning the involuntary servitude of Negroes or the involuntary patienthood of madmen is thus the most powerful justification possible of their enslavement and imprisonment. All other justifications of these policies are feeble in comparison. In fact, once the systematic oppression of one group by another becomes fully

---

* The first time the Constitution mentions slavery by name—that is, as "involuntary servitude"—is when, in 1865, the Thirteenth Amendment abolishing slavery is added to it. I can think of no better example to illustrate the point that no oppressive institution can be named correctly and survive; or, perhaps, no oppressive institution can be named correctly until after it has been overthrown.

articulated and is maintained by offering some sort of justification for it, its days are numbered. In the circular logic that appears to govern human affairs of this sort, if a practice is truly justifiable, no justification for it is offered; and if a justification is offered for it, it seems only to prove its fundamentally unjustifiable character. Perhaps this is something the French always knew, for their proverb warns that "Qui s'excuse, s'accuse" (He who excuses himself, accuses himself).

This primal justification by silence—by the tacit acceptance of act or practice, belief or ritual, as "obviously right"—seems to have its roots in language. Consider, in this connection, the Jewish injunction against naming God or forming any kind of image or representation of Him. This prohibition betrays a profound recognition of the role of language in enabling human beings to master their material and personal environment; a recognition, in other words, of the fact that to keep men and women in subjection to authority, it is necessary to obstruct their use of language.[3] Thus, an authority that justifies itself is no longer an absolute authority. Indeed, this is the way we distinguish between religious and scientific authorities.

Once the justification of no justification is relinquished, people resort to a few simple and quite consistent claims to legitimize what they do, especially when what they do is to harm another person or group. There are three main categories of such justifications. One is that "we" are human, but "they" are not. Both victimizer and victim may be nearly anyone or any group, but in Western history, as we know, the typical "they's" have been Jews, Negroes, witches, heretics, and madmen. After no justification at all, this is the next most powerful justification, since by transforming the victim from person to thing—the Jew to vermin, the Negro to chattel, the so-called mental patient to sick organism—he is immediately removed from the realm to which moral discourse normally applies.* Killing sick or aged cats or dogs is not something that legislators and jurists worry about. Thus, if we can metaphorize certain individuals or groups as animals—or as forms even lower on the evolutionary scale!—then we can practice treatment or euthanasia on them. If we want to feel really proud of ourselves, we can declare that our objects of solicitude have a right to treatment or to euthanasia. Our self-appointed right to treat and kill thus becomes their right to treatment and merciful death.

Another standard justification for victimization is for the victimizer to claim that "he" himself is a victim. Jew, Negro, witch, madman—each and every member of these groups has been said to constitute a threat to the ordinary, peace-loving citizen, whose duty it thus becomes to defend himself and his group against these enemies. This is a plausible justification for harmful acts, but it is much weaker than the two others we have considered, as it leaves the critical observer free to weigh the claims and counterclaims of the conflicting parties.

* In a recent criticism of my views, Moore makes just this point to support the psychiatric coercion of mental patients:

Since mental illness negates our assumptions of rationality, we do not hold the mentally ill responsible. It is not so much that we excuse them from a prima facie case of responsibility; rather, by being unable to regard them as fully rational beings, we cannot affirm the essential condition to viewing them as moral agents to begin with. In this the mentally ill join (to a decreasing degree) infants, wild beasts, plants, and stones—none of which are responsible because of the absence of any assumption of rationality.[4]

7

The fourth standard justification for victimization—now perhaps the most fashionable—is a peculiar refinement of the previous claim: "They" are a threat, not to "us," but to "themselves!" As the formula for self-defense grows out of the proposition that "they" are a threat to "us" because "they" are Jews or heretics, witches or madmen—so the formula for coerced treatment grows out of the proposition that "they" are a threat to "themselves," because they are inept or insane, poor or psychotic. This then justifies "our" ostensibly helping "them," while "we" remain securely in possession of the power to define and deploy our therapy. This tactic, originally theological but in recent centuries mainly therapeutic, is perhaps the most desperate, deceptive, and despicable of all the justifications for human victimization.[5] It is ironic that in its psychiatric application, it should now have the support of many of the most liberal elements of American society, including that of the American Civil Liberties Union.[6]

Although the principal justifications for human victimization lend themselves readily to division along the lines I have indicated, the categories so generated and named are not as discrete as they might seem. In fact, each of the tactics implies, and borrows from, those of the others. Thus, the dehumanization tactic implies threat, defense, and sometimes therapy; self-defense often merges into dehumanization; and therapy usually conceals both dehumanization and self-defense.

In the history of psychiatry, which is coeval with the history of involuntary mental hospitalization, the coercion of the madman by the mad-doctor has been justified in all of the ways listed above: that is, by silence, and by claims that the madman is subhuman, dangerous, and needs treatment. I have written extensively on these matters,

8

subjecting the justificatory rhetoric of psychiatry to special scrutiny. There is no need here to review the evidence which such an inquiry into the history and language of psychiatry produces. Suffice it to say that the attempt to justify involuntary mental hospitalization on the grounds of treatment is neither novel, as its present proponents pretend, nor, in my opinion, is it morally acceptable.[8]

Two wrongs do not make a right. It is wrong to deprive innocent people of liberty. But it is also wrong to try to set them free by acceding to the definition of the victims as patients, of the victimizers as psychiatrists, and of the control of former by the latter as diagnosis, hospitalization, and treatment.

In this book I shall use the Donaldson case to amplify and exemplify the view I have always held about commitment: namely, that in a society such as ours is and aspires to be, involuntary mental hospitalization is an unjustifiable moral and legal wrong. Hence, attempts to illegitimize it on the grounds that psychiatrists fail to treat involuntary mental patients is as faulty logically and as unworthy morally as are attempts to legitimize it on the grounds that psychiatrists protect society from madmen or madmen from themselves. Because each of these justifications is premised on the legitimacy of depriving innocent persons of their liberty under psychiatric auspices, supporting such justifications validate, implicitly but therefore all the more powerfully, the legitimacy of psychiatric coercion.

As the founders of our Republic rejected theological coercion, not in this or that particular application of it, but in principle—so, I submit, we ought to reject psychiatric coercion, not in this or that particular application of it, but in principle.

9

III

If we wish to raise our understanding of problems of psychiatry and law to an intellectually more satisfying level than that on which discussions of such problems are usually conducted, it is essential that we keep in mind the differences between explanations and justifications, and the principal rhetorical forms of justifying injury to others.

It is essential, also, that we recognize that the disjunction between avowed claims and actual conduct is crucial to the behavior of both madmen and mad-doctors—or, to use the contemporary vernacular, both mental patients and psychiatrists. For example, a person likely to be diagnosed as schizophrenic may declare: "I am the Messiah, God commands me to save the world, and to do so I must kill so-and-so." The patient's putative aim is to save the world, to do good. However, his actual conduct, as judged by the recipients of his benevolence, is deemed to be dangerous and harmful, with consequences all too familiar.

The situation with respect to the mad-doctor or institutional psychiatrist is much the same, with the roles reversed. He declares: "I am a doctor, my medical training and ethic command me that I help sick people, and to do so I must electroshock so-and-so." The doctor's putative aim is to help the patient, to treat him for his disease. However, his actual conduct, as judged by the recipients of his benevolence, is deemed to be not treatment but torture, with consequences again all too familiar.

Such disjunctions between putative aims and actual performances cannot long stand unresolved. In the modern world they are resolved, at least in the areas I am here considering, by the simple expedient of substituting authority for evidence. Thus, when the majority—when official science in alliance with the state—declare, as they do in the case of mad-doctoring, that the psychiatrist's actual performances are treatments consistent with his putative objectives of curing mental illness, the disjunction between the doctor's self-serving aims and his other-damaging acts is better than resolved: It is defined out of existence.

Similarly, when the majority declare, as they do in the case of madness, that the mental patient's putative objectives and his actual performances are the symptoms and signs of a medical disorder, the disturbing disjunction between his self-serving aims and his other-damaging acts is again better than resolved: It is defined out of existence. Henceforth, both of these disjunctions can be recognized and addressed only at the risk of insulting established professional beliefs and practices, and incurring the risks customarily accompanying such behavior.

Obviously, where the state is a party to this sort of psychiatric misrepresentation—where it is itself the agent or agency of fraud or force—it cannot also be the safeguard against its own action. This, then, is the fundamental political, ideological, and economic source of the difficulty that faces the contemporary critic of psychiatry. Countless psychiatric principles today are based on baldfaced lies—such as calling buildings in which innocent people are imprisoned hospitals. And countless psychiatric practices today consist of nothing but crass coercions—such as the incarceration of persons under psychiatric auspices called mental hospitalization. These dramatic disjunctions between putative objectives and actual performances, pervasive in institutional psychiatry, are now supported by church, state, and science. Accordingly, the psychiatric scholar's first task must be to reassert the evidence of his naked eyes and ears. For it is of little use to explain, justify, or modify policies that linguistically imply that certain propositions are true when they are actually false, and that socially authenticate aims as medical and technical when they are actually moral and political.

2

The Case
of Kenneth Donaldson

I

Kenneth Donaldson was incarcerated in the Florida State Hospital at Chattahoochee in January 1957 and was released in July 1971. His commitment was initiated by his father, who petitioned for it, and it was granted by a county judge sitting in Pinellas County, Florida.

If we want to come to grips with the actual human problems of commitment and mental hospitalization, it is necessary that we form an accurate picture of what happened in the Donaldson case (which is typical of countless such cases), and that we confront the human dilemmas it poses.

When Kenneth Donaldson arrived in Florida, in August 1956, he was forty-eight years old, divorced, and unemployed. For several months he lived with his parents, who resided at a trailer court, apparently uneventfully. In November of 1956, according to Bruce Ennis,* Donaldson "mentioned to his father that someone, perhaps one of the neighbors, might be putting something in his food."[1] Although Ennis says that Donaldson mentioned this idea to his parents, it might be more accurate to say that he complained to them, or that he accused the neighbors of poisoning him. These distinctions are important, as we cannot understand the interplay between so-called mental patients and others unless we recognize the paramount role of inflated self-importance and covert or overt coercion in the claims and conduct of the former, and of inflated self-importance and deceptive therapeutic counter-coercion in the claims and conduct of the latter.

Let us assume that the older Donaldson heard his son's idea about poisoning as an accusation or complaint. What could he do about it? This sort of complaint makes a person's loved ones wonderfully confused and helpless, which is, in my opinion, just what it is intended to do. There is also a hint, or more, in such a communication that Donaldson may have thought that *his parents* were poisoning him. After all, he was eating *their* food. The metaphoric meaning of madness is all too apparent in such communi-

---

* Bruce Ennis was chief counsel for Donaldson in his suit against O'Connor and argued his case before the Supreme Court. He is the Director of the New York Civil Liberties Union's Civil Liberties and Mental Illness Litigation Project, and Staff Counsel for the Mental Health Law Project.

14

cation, but this is a subject we cannot consider in detail here.[2] Suffice it to say, speculatively to be sure, that Donaldson was upsetting his parents by telling them, in effect, that he was not entirely happy to be in their home and was not exactly grateful for their support. Had the elder Donaldson been able to hear his son's message in this way and had he been able to free himself of the psychiatric prejudices of the day, he might have replied: "If you don't like it here, why don't you leave?" Had he done so, the *Donaldson* case as legal history would have ended before it began.

This is not the only thing that might have happened differently. For just as Donaldson's father had the option of separating himself from his son rather than committing him, so Donaldson himself had certain options which we cannot ignore.

If people live in a society where there are automobiles and traffic lights, or electricity and high tension lines, they will have some familiarity with the uses and dangers of these artifacts and the rules for using them. Similarly, if people live in a society where there are psychiatrists, commitment laws, and persons locked up in mental hospitals, then they will know something—some more, some less— about these things. In fact, Kenneth Donaldson knew quite a lot about psychiatry. Although Ennis does not mention it, Donaldson had been in a mental hospital once before: in 1943, he had spent three months in the Marcy State Hospital in Utica, New York. These facts are essential for our understanding of Donaldson's complicity in his own commitment and protracted confinement.*

* Indeed, the supposition that Kenneth Donaldson possessed more than the average amount of information on this subject is supported by Ennis himself: "Intelligent and articulate, Donaldson rapidly be-

It seems likely that when Donaldson told his father that someone was putting poison in his food, he knew that a possible—if not probable—outcome of such a communication was involuntary mental hospitalization. But regardless of whether or not Donaldson thought or knew what I am here imputing to him when he made his first complaints about poisoning to his father, he must surely have had some inkling about the reaction his communication was likely to provoke. There must have been some sort of verbal or nonverbal communication between the two Donaldsons after the son dropped the verbal bomb about poisoning in his father's lap. It seems inconceivable that during this period Donaldson had no inkling that his father was planning to commit him. Perhaps his father even threatened to do so. We simply do not know. All the records are silent about these events.

In short, there was a period before his commitment during which Donaldson had some options about whether to allow himself to be committed or not. According to Ennis, Donaldson first mentioned being poisoned to his father in late November. It was not until December 10 that the father filed a petition for a sanity hearing. During those weeks, had Donaldson wanted to avoid hospitalization, he could have stopped complaining about being poisoned, could have pleaded with his father not to commit him, or could have left his father's home and Florida, thus relieving his parents of the immediate emotional and practical pressure to commit him. Again, we do not know what happened then, but we may infer that Donaldson

---

came the 'scribe' and spokesman for his section [in the hospital]. In 1961, largely because of his documented complaints to public officials, the Florida legislature established a committee to investigate the hospital."[3]

16

made no serious attempt to avoid commitment. In view of his previous mental hospitalization, his non-resistance to commitment is significant; and so is his subsequent non-cooperation with the hospital authorities. To ignore that, in these ways, Donaldson asked to be treated as a psychiatric slave, is as absurd as to insist that because he did, it was justifiable to treat him as one.

II

Donaldson's own account of his hospitalization in Florida and of the events preceding it is consistent with the conjectures I have offered and will offer subsequently. To a *Washington Star* reporter, he gave the following explanation of what happened to him:

> Donaldson says his troubles began in 1943, when he was living in Syracuse. "I blacked out going home from work one night. I didn't know what the reason was. My father and my wife found me walking in the street in the morning. They asked me to go before the county judge, and he said there was no way he could commit me. But because I felt that I couldn't go back to work that night, he said I should sign myself in at the state observation center for 10 days, and I did."[4]

Donaldson here claims, first, that he "blacked out," using a symptom that is just as much an evasion as is the psychiatric diagnosis of schizophrenia; second, that he was hospitalized because of the actions of his father, wife, and the county judge, and not because of his own actions; and third, that he was sent to the hospital because he could not go to work. What is Donaldson's blacking out hiding here? In his book about his psychiatric experiences, Donaldson gives this account about how his difficulties began:

On a dreary winter morning in 1943, I stood before an Onondaga County judge in the stately courthouse of Syracuse, New York, before the regular session came to order. I was not a criminal. I was there to ask the judge's advice on a matter that had come up on my job at a defense plant. I had had some trouble and felt that I could not go back to work again. But the law said that I could not quit a defense job. The judge said it was a matter for the doctors. He advised me to sign myself in at a psychiatric observation center for ten days. On my decision voluntarily to place my fate in the hands of doctors lies the wreckage of my life, traumatizing everyone else in my family as well.[5]

Ironically, Donaldson's book is full of the most damaging evidence against many of his own claims and the claims of the Mental Health Law Project (MHLP) advanced on his behalf. For example, he reproduces an "Abstract of Commitment Paper," which gives his full name as "W. Kenneth," and states that he was admitted to the Marcy State Hospital on March 12, 1943 as a transfer from the Syracuse Psychopathic Hospital.[6] The petitioner for this commitment was Olive J. Donaldson, Kenneth Donaldson's wife, who stated that:

Patient has had a previous episode for which he was not hospitalized. In January 1943 he stated that he

18

was being followed and that people were after him. Patient believes that he has committed a serious crime and that the FBI is after him. He later said that the Government has provided Army and Navy men to look after him. Patient has run away from home on two occasions and has frequently talked about this.[7]

On March 11, 1943, just prior to his transfer to Marcy State Hospital, the examining physicians at the Syracuse Psychopathic Hospital made this note about Donaldson's mental condition: "Restless, overactive, shallow emotionally, affect at times inappropriate. . . . thought men were following him to kill him and that he was being protected by many men. . . . makes rather grandiose plans. . . ."[8]

What all this means is, to a large extent, a matter of conjecture, but surely it suggests that Donaldson was not happy at home and wanted to get away from it, and that at least partly as a result of his domestic and personal difficulties he ended up as a mental hospital patient.

In his interview with the *Washington Star*, Donaldson gave the following account of his hospitalization in Florida:

Donaldson was again locked up when he visited Florida. He thought it was because of a manuscript he had written criticizing mental institutions. He did not learn until $3\frac{1}{2}$ years later that his parents had asked that he be examined. "It said in my papers that I had been examined physically and mentally by two doctors and the deputy sheriff," Donaldson recalled. "But they came nowhere near

19

me. And for 15 years, doctors kept telling me I was crazy because I said I wasn't examined." [9]

It is worth noting that in his efforts to explain what happened to him, both here and elsewhere, Donaldson dwells on his previous hospitalization, which Ennis omits. And he omits his complaints about being poisoned, which Ennis cites as the reason for his commitment.

Donaldson's account of his life after his discharge from Marcy State Hospital is also inconsistent with Ennis's account of it. Ennis says that at the time of his commitment in Florida, Donaldson was unemployed. Donaldson says: "I drove my car home from [Marcy], went to work the next week, and never lost a day's work until I was put in Florida State Hospital in 1957."[10]

After his stay at Marcy, according to Donaldson, his life was ruined by the stigma of being an ex-mental patient. He attributes his divorce and also his frequent changes of jobs to it. But this cloud had a silver lining: As a result of his psychiatric experiences, Donaldson found his calling. Henceforth he would devote his life to crusading for the rights of mental patients. He started to write a book "as my only means of exposing the harassment and thus hopefully putting an end to it. Before the book was completed, I went to Florida for a visit with my parents. From there I mailed the manuscript to the *Saturday Evening Post*. . . . Three days later I landed in the 'hole' of the Pinellas County Jail in Clearwater on a writ of Inquisition of Incompetency."[11]

Before his commitment to the Florida State Hospital, Donaldson was in no position to get very far in his chosen career as a psychiatric reformer. His confinement, release, and litigation changed all that. Propped up by the Mental Health Law Project as one of its favorite "victims," and he in turn propping up the MHLP as one of its star claimants, in 1975 both Donaldson and the MHLP emerged on the scene as the leading mental health reformers in the United States.

III

The county judge who committed Donaldson told him "that he was being sent to the hospital for a 'few weeks' to take some of this new medication, after which the judge said that he was certain that Donaldson would be 'all right' and would 'come back here.' "[12]

Clearly, the person most responsible for Donaldson's commitment was Donaldson's own father, who petitioned for it; and the second most responsible person was the county judge, who not only committed Donaldson but also misled him, to put it mildly. It is, in fact, unnecessary for a person to be in a hospital—full-time, and under lock and key—just to take pills. Indeed, one might go further and say that a hospital, especially a mental hospital, is precisely the one place in American society where a person cannot take pills; pills are there given to him.

The committing judge's remark about "new medication" is a classic example of the justificatory rhetoric of institutional psychiatry. What the judge said to Donaldson sounds good, and it probably made both the judge and Donaldson's father feel better about what they were doing. In reality, Donaldson was committed because he acted "crazy" and was officially adjudged to be "crazy." What justified his commitment, from the point of view of traditional psychiatry, was his mental illness—which had to be serious enough to warrant involuntary hospitalization. According to the psychiatrists, it was indeed serious enough: "Soon thereafter [admission, Donaldson] was diagnosed as a 'paranoid schizophrenic.' "[13]

The cardinal characteristics of paranoid schizophrenia are, first, that the patient makes claims about himself or the world with which psychiatrists and the society they represent disagree; and second, that the patient insists that he is normal or sane, whereas the psychiatrists and the society they represent insist that he is crazy or insane.[14] Kenneth Donaldson displayed both of these symptoms of paranoid schizophrenia in their most flagrant forms: He claimed that he was being poisoned, while the psychiatrists knew that he was not; and he claimed that he was mentally healthy, while the psychiatrists knew that he was mentally sick. It is important to keep these claims and counter-claims in mind, for they form the frame into which considerations of Donaldson's non-treatment must be placed before they can be properly understood or judged.

Since Donaldson's suit was brought on the ground that he was denied treatment for his mental illness, a treatment to which he had a supposed constitutional right, the facts surrounding his illness and non-treatment are of the greatest importance. Although Donaldson had ostensibly been committed for treatment, Judge Wisdom of the Court of Appeals emphasized that: "Donaldson received no commonly accepted psychiatric treatment. Shortly after his first mental examination, Donaldson, a Christian Scientist, refused to take any medication or to submit to electroshock treatments, and he consistently refused to submit to either of these forms of therapy. No other therapy was offered."[15]

Did Donaldson refuse to submit to these treatments because he was a Christian Scientist or because he did not consider himself to be mentally sick? As I shall show in a moment, Donaldson had, throughout his hospitalization, advanced both of these grounds for his objection to psychiatric treatments.

Donaldson's claimed adherence to the religion of Christian Science has been consistently underplayed or ignored in considerations of this case. As a Christian Scientist, Donaldson was entitled, under the First Amendment, to the practice of his religion. One of the things that the doctrine of Christian Science teaches is the rejection of doctors and medical treatment. Thus, as a Christian Scientist, Donaldson's most basic right in the state hospital lay not in any fictitious right to treatment, but in the very real right to reject treatment.*

Once in the hospital, Donaldson chose to exercise his right as a Christian Scientist.** And the psychiatrists chose to respect his right. For this Judge Wisdom punished them: "At trial, Gumanis mentioned 'recreational' and 'religious' therapy as forms of therapy given Donaldson; but this amounted to allowing Donaldson to attend

---

* In 1971, a U.S. Court of Appeals ruled in favor of a woman, a Christian Scientist, who sued Bellevue Hospital in New York City on the ground that while involuntarily hospitalized, she was given medication against her will. Her claim was upheld on the ground that she had a "constitutional right to refuse medical treatment because of religious beliefs."[16]

** In his claim against O'Connor, Donaldson actually advanced two alternative arguments, namely, that he should have been treated or released, and that he was not a person properly subject to involuntary mental hospitalization and treatment. The courts holding for Donaldson seemed to give some weight to both of these claims, making a logically incisive analysis of the case virtually impossible.

Church and to engage in recreational activities, privileges he probably would have been allowed in a prison." [17]

The court's stance here is remarkable: It puts the words "recreational" and "religious" modifying therapy between quotation marks, although it never puts the term "electroshock" qualifying therapy between quotation marks. This means either that it considers religion and recreation as totally non-therapeutic, but considers electroshock to be therapeutic—which is moronic; or that it downgrades these common-sense procedures as insignificant or useless——which is malevolent. The court's branding prayer and play as non-therapeutic because they might be allowed in prison is also peculiar. By this reasoning, if a myopic is allowed glasses in prison, or a diabetic insulin, then corrective lenses and injections of insulin also are not therapeutic.

Furthermore, the evidence is clear that Donaldson rejected treatment on two separate grounds—because he was a Christian Scientist and because he was not ill. Nowhere in the presentation or litigation of this case are these two grounds clearly identified, and nowhere is it emphasized that they strongly support one another and Donaldson's fundamental rejection of himself as a patient and of his captors as his doctors.

In his anonymous contribution to the Georgetown Symposium on the Right to Treatment, Donaldson emphasizes his rejection of the patient role on the ground that he was not ill: "I came to this state from the North as a visitor in August 1956. There was nothing wrong with me mentally, morally, physically, financially, or legally. . . . Yet, without any examination by anybody, I was declared sick."[18]

Nevertheless, in his suit against O'Connor and Gumanis,

the psychiatrists in charge of him at the Florida State Hospital, the crux of Donaldson's claim was that he was deprived of his "constitutional right to treatment," a claim the trial judge accepted and incorporated into his instructions to the jury.[19] The judge underscored his acceptance of this "right" by also telling the jury that "the purpose of involuntary hospitalization is treatment. . . . Without such treatment there is no justification from a constitutional standpoint for continued confinement." [20] Although defining involuntary treatment as a constitutional right is patent nonsense, it is especially absurd in a case where the patient is a Christian Scientist who steadfastly denies that he is ill and needs treatment.*

It is ironic that Donaldson successfully maintained his integrity against his psychiatric "enemies," to whom he never acknowledged his need for psychiatric treatment, only to lose it to his legal "friends," to whom he eagerly conceded his need for it.** No sooner was he released, after having resisted confessing mental illness to psychiatrists O'Connor and Gumanis, than he turned around and, in effect, confessed it to attorneys Birnbaum and Ennis:

* As a Christian Scientist, Donaldson consistently refused the treatment offered him at the Florida State Hospital. His legal posture is thus like that of a Catholic woman who refuses an abortion, and then sues the doctors for not having aborted her. I cannot judge the MHLP's intentions or motives in doing what it did with Donaldson. But I insist that, especially in the morally murky waters of legal psychiatry, those who strive for freedom from psychiatric coercion cannot afford to use their adversaries' immoral methods for achieving their own aims.

** According to Donaldson himself, "The principal treatment [in the hospital] is brainwashing, consisting of lies . . . intended to bring the inmate to his knees, i.e., to a confession of 'mental illness.' After the confession, the inmate is in line for consideration for release. No confession, no release. . . ."[21]

He allowed his lawyers to litigate on the basis that he was deprived of treatment that he needed for his mental illness! The moral of this distasteful lesson is that institutional psychiatrists, in order to justify their diagnosis and confinement of the patients, refuse to release mental patients unless they confess to having been mentally ill; and that right-to-treatment lawyers—in order to justify their claims for the patients' therapeutic deprivations—refuse to champion mental patients unless they confess to having needed treatment for mental illness.

IV

How did Donaldson gain his release from the hospital? The circumstances surrounding his discharge are revealing. During his 14½ years of confinement, Donaldson petitioned for his freedom, unsuccessfully, through numerous writs of habeas corpus. According to Morton Birnbaum:*

[O]n 18 separate occasions, [Donaldson's] claims were presented to various Florida and federal courts, including the U.S. Supreme Court on four separate occasions. Through the last adverse decision by the Supreme Court in 1970, no court granted his petition for a writ of habeas corpus in spite of the fact that from 1969 on, he had had town privileges so that he could go back and forth into Chattahoochee at will.[22]

During the last two years of his hospitalization, Donaldson could thus have easily escaped, or "eloped," as psy-

* Morton Birnbaum, a general practitioner and lawyer, represented Donaldson while he was a patient at the Florida State Hospital. Birnbaum is the Executive Director of the Center for Law and Health Care Policy, New York City.

26

chiatrists put it. But he didn't. Nor was he discharged, although it seems that the hospital authorities were ready to let him go, provided he left on their terms. Moreover, although Donaldson claimed that he wanted to be free, evidently he wanted to be free only on his own terms. For many years, the relationship between O'Connor and Donaldson thus closely resembled that of a married couple seeking a divorce but unable to agree on the terms for it, each insisting on his or her complete innocence and demanding that a judge settle their dispute.[23] In an unhappy marriage, husband and wife often make demands on each other that each refuses to fulfill; in particular, each often asks the other to leave instead of himself or herself leaving. Similarly, during many years of Donaldson's "incarceration," keeper and kept were making demands on each other that each refused to fulfill. "Why do you want to stay and fight, when you could be free?" Donaldson quotes "Miss F.," a hospital social worker, asking him. His reply: "I didn't ask for this. I didn't choose the nuthouse for a career."[24] Actually, he did just that.*

* During the better part of his long period of "hospitalization," Donaldson could easily have gained his liberty if he had compromised on his principles. O'Connor and Gumanis evidently felt that they had met Donaldson half way by acceding to his requests to abstain from giving him treatments he did not want. In turn, they demanded that, like other patients, Donaldson be discharged by being signed out and by going to staff, conditions which, like the "treatments," Donaldson refused to accept.

For example, in 1966 Donaldson's daughter came to the hospital and wanted to sign him out. Donaldson refused to see her. "I explained to my children," he writes, "that I'm not going to be subjected to indignities ladled out by a bunch of goddammed mammyjamming honey-dippers. . . . If I gave one inch and let my daughter sign me out, I would lose the whole case against institutional psychiatry, for then the doctors could say they had cured me and let me go."[25] Similarly, when a friend came to the hospital to take

Why was Donaldson released when he was? The illness and treatment rhetoric would lead one to believe either that he received some effective therapy shortly before release or that he made some spontaneous progress toward recovery. There is not a shred of evidence that either occurred. Nor did anyone associated with the case make such a claim. Actually, Donaldson's release had no direct relationship to either Donaldson or his captors. It was brought about by changes in the psychiatric-political climate and fresh legal support for his cause.[27]

In the years preceding Donaldson's release, federal appellate courts had handed down several decisions limiting the grounds for psychiatric incarceration, and touting the notion of a right to treatment as a newly discovered constitutional right for involuntary mental patients. In the meantime, Donaldson had gained the support of the American Civil Liberties Union, which had long crusaded for better commitment laws, and which now embraced Donaldson as a promising test case.

The change in the power positions of the *dramatis personae* governing Donaldson's fate is revealed by the fact that while still a hospital inmate, he collaborated with his lawyers in bringing a class action suit on behalf of all patients in the hospital's ward where he himself was confined.[28] No patient who has been diagnosed as schizophrenic and locked up for fourteen years can do such a thing unless he has powerful friends, indeed, in the legal profession. Donaldson had made such friends, and they

---

him with him, he insisted that the psychiatrists let him go without going to staff, and when they refused to do so, he stayed in the hospital.[26] The result was five more years of jousting between patient and doctor, each trying to bring the other to his knees—and five more years of hospitalization or incarceration.

were "springing" him from the madhouse—albeit not without using him for their own purposes.

V

In his class action suit, Donaldson asked for damages and for habeas corpus relief for all members of the class. In July 1971 just two weeks before this suit was scheduled for argument before a federal court, Kenneth Donaldson received an unconditional discharge from the Florida State Hospital. *"Res ipsa loquitur":* The thing speaks for itself. Obviously, Donaldson was released from psychiatric confinement, not because he had suddenly become mentally healthy, nor because he had suddenly become non-dangerous, but because subjecting the legitimacy of his continued psychiatric incarceration to such a test was, under the new circumstances, deemed too risky by the legal-psychiatric authorities in charge of his case. Thus, the two most suggestive sets of facts about the Donaldson case—namely, those surrounding his commitment and his discharge—have been the two things most conspicuously ignored in all the briefs filed in this case and in all the judicial decisions rendered about it.

What happened after Donaldson was released? His petition for release suddenly became moot. The District Court accordingly dismissed the class action suit.[29] Donaldson's legal champions thereupon filed an amended complaint, alleging that the psychiatrists in charge of Donaldson "acted in bad faith toward plaintiff and with intentional, malicious, and reckless disregard of his constitutional rights."[30] The complaint sought $100,000 in damages on behalf of Donaldson.

The trial began on November 21, 1972 and lasted four

days. Donaldson's attorneys set out to prove, among other things, that "the defendants confined plaintiff against his will, knowing that he was not mentally ill or dangerous, and knowing that if mentally ill he was not receiving treatment for his mental illness."[31] They succeeded in proving this. Two of the defendant psychiatrists, O'Connor and Gumanis, were found personally guilty of depriving Donaldson of his liberty—thanks to the instructions the trial judge gave to the jury.* Two of his key instructions were:

> You are instructed that a person who is involuntarily civilly committed to a mental hospital does have a constitutional right to receive such individual treatment as will give him a realistic opportunity to be cured or to improve his mental condition.
>
> The purpose of involuntary mental hospitalization is treatment. . . . Without such treatment there is no justification, from a constitutional standpoint, for continued confinement.[32]

Donaldson was committed unjustly. Everyone who is committed is, in my opinion, committed unjustly. I submit, however, that Donaldson's psychiatrists were tried unjustly. The judge who presided over the trial ordered the jury to bring in what was in effect a directed verdict against the defendants. It did so, awarding Donaldson $17,000 in compensatory damages and $5,000 in punitive damages against O'Connor, and $11,500 in compensatory damages and $5,000 in punitive damages against Gumanis.[33]

---

* This judgment was not upheld by the Supreme Court and was remanded to the lower courts for reconsideration (see pages 79–80).

30

The view that Donaldson's so-called constitutional right to treatment was the crux of the issue in trial court is supported by the initial summary statement of the case by the Fifth Circuit Court of Appeals: "This case," wrote Judge Wisdom, "requires us to decide for the first time the far-reaching question whether the Fourteenth Amendment guarantees a right to treatment to persons involuntarily civilly committed to state mental hospitals. . . . Donaldson contends that he had a constitutional right to receive treatment or be released from the state hospital."[34]

After a review of the facts of the case, the Court of Appeals held "that the Fourteenth Amendment guarantees involuntarily civilly committed mental patients a right to treatment, and that the evidence was sufficient to support the verdict. . . . Accordingly, we affirm the judgment in Donaldson's favor."[35]

Besides emphasizing and re-emphasizing how Donaldson "received no commonly accepted psychiatric treatment," the Court cited, with unqualified approval, many authorities who support the doctrine of a right to treatment." [36] The first case cited was *Rouse* v. *Cameron*,[37] one of Judge David Bazelon's signal contributions to the advancement of the Therapeutic State.*

* There is a remarkable similarity between the *Rouse* and the *Donaldson* decisions that is worth noting here—namely, that in both cases judges intoxicated with the religion of psychiatry claimed not only that involuntarily hospitalized mental patients had a right to treatment but also insisted that, specifically, an individual who claimed to be well and who rejected treatment had such a right. Dissenting from Chief Judge Bazelon's opinion in the *Rouse* case, Judge Danaher sagely observed that the majority "are deciding a case which is not before us. In the first place, this appellant . . . was contending on his pleadings and at the trial that he was not insane and that he needed no treatment. His own expert, Dr. Marland, testified that Rouse was not mentally ill. . . ."[38] In short,

31

VI

I have long maintained that commitment is a response to a problem of housing rather than to a problem of illness.[39] At the time of his commitment, Donaldson was a homeless man—forty-eight years old, unemployed, living with his aged parents. It requires no great leap of the imagination to see that this living arrangement might have been something less than ideal for Donaldson and his parents. But none of them faced this dilemma directly. All agreed to disguise it as a problem of mental illness. The father filed a petition to have his son declared incompetent and to commit him to the state hospital; mother and son went along unprotestingly. Once arraigned, Donaldson did ask for a lawyer, and he pretended in other ways to protest his commitment. But these were mere dramatic gestures. In fact, he went along: He cooperated fully in the transfer of his residence from his father's home to the state hospital.

I submit that whatever its purported aims, justifications, or rationalizations might have been, Donaldson's original commitment was a solution to his problem of homelessness. Once we see this, we can formulate the moral problem it poses: Is compulsory housing a proper remedy for such a problem? I say that in a free society it is not. Housing qua housing may, and perhaps should, be offered

---

Bazelon's "landmark" decision in the *Rouse* case rested on the paradoxical premise that the government psychiatrists at St. Elizabeth's Hospital who were denying patients such as Rouse their right to treatment were, nevertheless, well qualified to determine whether or not the inmates in their captivity were mentally ill and hence in need of treatment.

to persons so disabled; but they should be left free to reject such offers and to suffer the consequences.

What about the needs of those who want to remove members of their household (or others) from their homes (or society) by rehousing them in mental hospitals? In a free society, they should not have such an option. Were the option of commitment removed from society, persons disturbed by so-called mental patients would have to choose frankly between living with them or "divorcing" them. The problem of justifying civil commitment would then never arise.

If there was one thing on which all the participants in the Donaldson case agreed, it was to avoid dealing with, or even mentioning, the basic issues underlying Donaldson's incarceration. The efficacy of this method of dealing with problems depends, as does the efficacy of so much else in human affairs, on whether or not others cooperate with it. If they do—if many or all concerned with an embarrassing or painful problem are happy to solve it by changing the subject—then denial works. The Donaldson case embodies and exemplifies the desire of psychiatrists, judges, and the public in general to look away from the embarrassing and painful problems of involuntary psychiatry—and gaze instead at the heart-warming sight of the right to treatment.

3

The Brief
for Donaldson

I

After the Court of Appeals for the Fifth Circuit upheld Donaldson's damage award, O'Connor appealed to the Supreme Court. How did Donaldson, a penniless ex-mental patient, support his court battles? In the way that is typical of litigation of this sort in modern American law: by being adopted as a test case by a powerful group waging its own crusade for social reform through court action. In Donaldson's case, the supporting organization was the Mental Health Law Project. Since the litigation of such test cases reveals as much about the interests and intentions of the individuals and groups that sponsor and support it as it does about the merits of the victim's case, it is necessary that we extend our scrutiny of the *Donaldson* case to the Mental Health Law Project itself, with special emphasis on its position on involuntary mental hospitalization; on the brief its lawyers filed, ostensibly for Donaldson; and on the implications—legal, logical and moral—of the arguments set forth in the brief.

According to its own definition, the Mental Health Law Project is "an interdisciplinary public-interest organization devoted to protecting the legal rights of the mentally handicapped (and those so labeled) and improving conditions for their care, treatment, education, and community life."[1]

Because of my interest in language and because I believe that words are as important to psychiatry as numbers are to arithmetic, I first want to offer a brief remark about the MHLP's name.[2] Names are, after all, symbols that persons bestow on themselves, others, and what they do; hence, names often reveal a great deal about who people are and what they do. If we assume that the originators of the MHLP named their organization truthfully, we would have to conclude that it is a law project *for* mental health *not against* involuntary psychiatry. By combining "mental health" and "law" in the name of this project, its founders and directors imply that they consider mental health as real or as substantial as law. Furthermore, by using the term mental health, they imply that it is something distinguishable from mental illness, a term that, in turn, leads them to support, however tacitly, the idea that mental illness is an illness that may be treated and cured by means of medical treatments. In my opinion, every one of these beliefs and premises hinders rather than helps the cause of diminishing and abolishing the present-day, legally legitimized victimization of people in the name of mental health. In fact, these beliefs and premises may, whether wittingly or otherwise, lead the members and supporters of the MHLP to promote the very evils they ostensibly oppose.

The Mental Health Law Project was established in 1972 by three sponsors—the American Civil Liberties Union Foundation (ACLU), the American Orthopsychiatric Association (AOA), and the Center for Law and Social Policy (an organization supported by the Ford Foundation). Headquartered in Washington, D.C., the project employs ten attorneys, headed by Paul R. Friedman, and four legal assistants. Its board of trustees covers a broad spectrum of personalities, from ex-mental patients active in patient liberation work to prominent institutional psychiatrists responsible for directing programs for involuntarily hospitalizing and treating mental patients. One of the psychiatrists on the MHLP's board of trustees is June Jackson Christmas, M.D., the Commissioner of the New York City Department of Mental Health and Mental Retardation Services. In that capacity, Christmas probably is responsible for more involuntary psychiatric confinements per year than any other psychiatrist in the world. Another psychiatrist on the board is Harold Visotsky, M.D., now the chairman of the Department of Psychiatry at Northwestern University School of Medicine in Chicago and formerly (from 1959 to 1969) the Director of the Illinois Department of Mental Health. Like Christmas, Visotsky is an institutional psychiatrist, in the strictest sense of that term: His ideological and economic loyalties always have been, and continue to be, to psychiatric institutions, not to individuals incarcerated in those institutions.

Indeed, the views expressed in the MHLP's official newsletter make it clear that this organization is self-consciously devoted to improving psychiatric slavery and to opposing efforts to abolish it. For example, in an editorial on the "Principle of the Least Restrictive Alternative," Paul Friedman, the managing attorney of the MHLP, comes down squarely in favor of both involuntary mental hospitalization and involuntary psychiatric treatment. Noting that competent mental patients "may" have a right to refuse treatment they do not want, he raises the question, "But what about incompetent residents?" and answers it as follows:

> When a mentally handicapped person is incompetent to give truly informed consent, there must be some form of substitute decision-making. But because hazardous or intrusive procedures may infringe on fundamental . . . rights, additional protections—such as review by an independent "human rights committee"—are needed to insure that such substituted decisions are in the "best interests" of the person. . . . For example, . . . [for] a severely disturbed mental patient, verbal psychotherapy should be tried before ECT is contemplated.[3]

This, of course, is only a slightly retouched form of a position long held by institutional psychiatry. Behind the high-sounding phrases, there remains the unequivocal approval of electroshock treatment for individuals without their consent but for their "best interests," as that interest

37

is determined by the individual's judicial and psychiatric adversaries.

A statement written by Joel Klein, one of the MHLP's staff attorneys, makes the project's position on involuntary mental hospitalization crystal clear. "My concern," writes Klein, addressing himself specifically to those who would outlaw psychiatric slavery "is that one result of abolishing involuntary commitment will be to ignore the legitimate treatment needs of some people who require care."[4] Speaking for the MHLP in its official newsletter, Klein thus identifies himself as another true believer in the religion of psychiatry: Mental illness is an illness that requires treatment, especially when the patient has no insight into his own need for it. "First," explains Klein, as if he had just discovered this idea himself, "there are people who, precisely because of severe mental illness, will not accept treatment voluntarily. For example, some depressed people believe they are unworthy of help."[5] From this Klein concludes that, "If effective treatment can be provided within a reasonably short period, I believe that sound social policy should allow for a limited curtailment of civil liberties to permit it."[6] Actually, the position here advocated is even more repressive than that of traditional institutional psychiatry—inasmuch as it supports involuntary mental hospitalization not because the patient is dangerous but because it affords his captors an opportunity to give him the treatment:

[P]ragmatic reasons lead me to conclude that involuntary commitment should be accepted in limited circumstances. Involuntary patients arguably have a constitutional right to treatment, as several courts

38

already have held. Thus, once a patient is committed, his lawyer can use the courts to insure that treatment is provided.[7]

Klein's logic and the MHLP's true aims could hardly be more clearly stated: Because involuntary mental patients have a right to treatment but voluntary mental patients do not, the road to psychiatric reform lies through involuntary hospitalization and the involuntary treatment it makes possible. Here it is, right from the pages of the MHLP's "Summary of Activities":

[I]t seems extremely unlikely that voluntary patients will soon be found to have a constitutional right to treatment. Rather, when indigent, they must accept whatever services a state provides—usually significantly less than needed. In short, the irony is that people who want mental treatment frequently cannot get it, while those who do not want it sometimes can. I cannot overemphasize that in the absence of involuntary commitment it will be extremely difficult to force the state to provide decent mental health care.[8]

Such, then, are the psychiatric positions of the organization that used Donaldson as its celebrated test case. In Klein's own words, the central aim of the MHLP is to *force* the state to provide involuntary psychiatric treatment for involuntary patients. This aim is not merely different from that of *forcing* the state to free its involuntary mental patients but is antithetical to it: For if there are no involuntary patients, there are no persons with a right to mental treatment, an outcome that would place the MHLP's goal of providing more and better involuntary mental treatment utterly beyond reach.

II

The character of the organizations that have brought the MHLP into being and support it, and their record on psychiatry, raise equally serious questions about the true aims of this group. As an organization sponsored by the ACLU, the AOA, and the Ford Foundation, the MHLP is an odd alliance, indeed. The American Orthopsychiatric Association is, in fact, one of the several American unions for the protection and promotion of institutional psychiatry. Founded in 1924 by Karl Menninger, its explicit aim was to bring together the "representatives of the neuropsychiatric or medical view of crime."[9] The name of the organization itself betokens a lack of interest in, and respect for, civil liberties or human rights—as the very term "orthopsychiatry" implies the belief that crime is a medical problem, and that physicians are a morally, politically, and scientifically chosen elite whose duty it is to straighten out the crooked behavior of their fellow men and women.[10]

Before World War I, the American Orthopsychiatric Association celebrated the glories of involuntary mental hospitalization by singing its praises in choirs conducted by such pioneer therapeutic totalitarians as Gregory Zilboorg. "The law," declared Zilboorg, "has never been neglectful of the so-called insane. In civil law, it is extremely lenient; it commits an individual to the mental institution with the greatest reasonableness and with the minimum of difficulties. . . ."[11]

Since then, the American Orthopsychiatric Association has more than lived up to its original mandate. For example, among its recent presidents was Judge David Bazelon, a prominent proponent of civil commitment and the right to treatment.[12]

The American Civil Liberties Union's psychiatric record also leaves much to be desired. During the first few decades of its existence, the ACLU took no notice of psychiatry and involuntary mental hospitalization. Once it did, however, it immediately embraced it as an answer to the problems of social deviance and social control. In his adulatory history of the ACLU, Charles Markmann relates how, toward the end of World War II, the Union "began to draft model statutes for the commitment of the insane. . . . Twenty years after the first Union draft of a model bill for commitments to mental hospitals, Congress enacted for the District of Columbia a law closely following the Union's proposals."[13]

The Union thus has a long history of uncritically accepting the concept of mental illness, whose treatment by imprisonment is casually delegated to the psychiatric profession. Although in recent years the ACLU has made some ambivalent attempts to confront the realities of involuntary psychiatry, its position on the issue of commitment has remained pro-psychiatry and anti-civil liberties.[14] This may be owing partly to the influence of its two most prominent psychiatric-judicial experts, Karl Menninger and Ramsey Clark. Clark's views on commitment can be conveyed by means of a single quotation:

Where commitment is necessary, civil commitment of a contractual nature offers the opportunity for physical control over the addict without the stigma of a conviction for crime. Voluntary participation, which is the basis for civil commitment,[*] creates an attitude helpful in achieving a cure.[16]

This pro-commitment view is not limited to a few psychiatrically biased individuals in the ACLU. As recently as 1972,

The ACLU Board of Directors [was] still polishing its policy on mental commitments. However, most of the Union's leaders appear to agree on certain minimal standards: Involuntary commitment should be the last resort to which society turns in dealing with the mentally impaired. Before commitment there must be clear demonstration that the individual is a danger to himself or herself or to others. . . . And there must be assurance that the individual who is committed will, in fact, be treated adequately.[17]

Perhaps the most telling evidence for the view that the ACLU is still inimical to the civil rights of mental patients is, ironically, furnished by Donaldson himself in his autobiographical account of his psychiatric calvary. Recalling a conversation he had with Birnbaum at the Florida State Hospital shortly before his release, Donaldson writes that Birnbaum told him: "I delayed filing because the American Civil Liberties blew hot and cold. They keep asking

---

* Clark's view of civil commitment as voluntary is similar to the Soviet view of it.[15] It is fitting that this Orwellian touch should be added to the history of mad-doctoring by Communist psychiatry and by the chairman of the ACLU's National Advisory Council.

what your politics are. I'm a member myself and I keep telling them what's the difference, he's incarcerated unconstitutionally. Finally, I told them I would proceed without them. But they definitely are in now."[18]

Thus, judging from the loyalties of the individuals and groups composing the MHLP, we would have to conclude that, at best, it is an organization for promoting mental health reform in the tradition of Dorothea Dix; or that, at worst, it is an organization for opposing the thrust of the abolitionist sentiment now growing in the United States with respect to mental health legislation. The latter inference is suggested by the fact that the MHLP's work deflects attention from the actual wrongs of involuntary mental hospitalization to the alleged wrongs of inadequate or insufficient psychiatric treatment for involuntary mental patients.

It is essential that we keep these facts about the AOA, the ACLU, and the MHLP in mind when we try to understand the historical background and the legal-political context of the *Donaldson* case. Donaldson's was truly a test case, with Kenneth Donaldson himself as the guinea pig. The claims and counterclaims in the case and the judicial rulings about it were the trials and errors of the experimenters. The results of these experiments have nothing to do with Donaldson or, for that matter, any other person. They show us only the forces of the psychiatric imperialists, in effect demanding explicit judicial sanctions for psychiatric slavery through the articulation of a constitutional right to treatment, and the forces of the defenders of the psychiatric status quo, concealing their coercions behind traditional judicial authorizations for the smooth management of the psychiatric plantations.

III

After setting forth the facts of the case and the fate of the litigation to date, the MHLP brief continues as follows:

Respondent . . . was confined expressly for the purpose of receiving treatment for his alleged mental illness. Petitioner knew that respondent was not receiving *any* treatment, and that he was receiving only the custodial care he would have received in a prison. . . . Petitioner had the authority to release respondent from the hospital, but instead allowed his confinement to continue for nearly fifteen years.[19]

Except for the statement that O'Connor "had the authority to release" Donaldson, the foregoing assertions are simply not true. Donaldson was not confined expressly for the purpose of receiving treatment. He was confined because he was officially diagnosed as a paranoid schizophrenic who was adjudged to be dangerous to himself and others. Nevertheless, the MHLP's brief also claims that "petitioner knew that respondent was not dangerous to himself or to others, and that respondent was capable of providing for his basic needs in the community."[20]

It is not clear how the attorneys who wrote this could in good conscience assert that O'Connor *knew* all these things. It is an integral part of psychiatry as the "science" of the human mind that paranoid schizophrenics are dangerous. Just as true believers in Judaism believe that Jews are the Chosen People, and true believers in Christianity believe that Jesus is God, so true believers in psychiatry believe that paranoid schizophrenia is an identifiable

44

mental disease and that those who suffer from it are dangerous. The MHLP's brief does not challenge psychiatry as a fake science. Nor does it claim that O'Connor was anything but a true believer in psychiatry. Thus, by imputing beliefs to O'Connor that O'Connor presumably does not hold, probably never held, and, in principle, could not possibly have held, the attorneys for the MHLP do him the same injustice that institutional psychiatrists do their victims: they accuse him and condemn him by claiming that certain unsupported derogatory conjectures are "facts."

Actually, the MHLP's brief for Donaldson is so repugnant—in its claim for a right to treatment for a patient who consistently maintained that he was not sick and did not want any treatment, and who, to boot, was a Christian Scientist; in its tendentious citation of supporting evidence; and in singling out O'Connor as the devil in the drama while wholly neglecting the role of the courts in consistently authorizing and reauthorizing Donaldson's detention—that it can only compound a fair-minded observer's distaste for institutional psychiatry and its diagnoses with an equally intense distaste for the MHLP and its advocacy of a right to treatment.

In their argument, the MHLP attorneys cite the Court's statement in *Jackson* v. *Indiana*, that "the States have traditionally exercised broad power to commit persons found to be mentally ill."[21] This statement raises an obvious question: If the state has such power, how can O'Connor be faulted for keeping someone in his hospital who, the courts have repeatedly told him, is insane and should be confined? Ignoring this question, the MHLP brief jumps, without hesitation or evidence, from the broad power of the states to commit to the narrow but important ques-

45

tion which it claims the *Donaldson* case poses: namely, the right to treatment or release. In reality, this question is posed not by the merits of this case but by the MHLP.

IV

The *Donaldson* case is very troubling for several reasons, of which the MHLP's posture toward it is only one. Another reason is that, at least according to one legal commentator, Donaldson's original commitment was illegal. In an article written shortly before the Supreme Court handed down its decision, Brian Schwartz noted that Donaldson's confinement "violated Florida law, which limited involuntary commitment to persons resident in Florida for at least one year, whereas Donaldson had been in Florida for only four months. The examining physicians had erroneously reported that Donaldson had been in Florida for four years."[22]

The attorneys for the MHLP must have known this. Why, then, did they concentrate their legal firepower on a suit claiming a right to treatment instead of on one asserting false imprisonment? This rhetorical question suggests, too, that the MHLP does not want to abolish slavery but wants to improve the plantations.

One wonders, too, if Donaldson knew that his original confinement was illegal, not just for the reasons he had advanced, but simply because he was not a Florida resident. And if he knew it, why did he permit his lawyers to base their litigation on the premise that his commitment was legal?

Sidestepping the issues of why Donaldson was committed and whether his commitment was legal, the MHLP comes down squarely for a plea for a right to treatment:

"The most critical of the post-confinement rights—the right to be restored to liberty either by treatment or else by release—has been recognized and endorsed by medical experts, by legal commentators, and by the United States."[23] One of the groups cited under the heading of such medical experts is the American Psychiatric Association (APA). In fact, the APA was opposing, not supporting, Donaldson.[24] By making common cause with precisely those psychiatric and legal authorities most responsible for involuntary psychiatric interventions, Donaldson and his champions vitiate both their arguments and their credibility. A few facts about the APA and its position on commitment must suffice here.

In 1844, thirteen superintendents of mental hospitals joined to form the Association of Medical Superintendents of American Institutions for the Insane, the organization that became, in 1921, the APA. The original name of this first American psychiatric organization is revealing, and so is its first official resolution. The group's name articulated its character: it was an organization of "medical superintendents," that is, of physicians who were in charge of incarcerated individuals considered and called insane. The organization's first official proposition was: "Resolved, that it is the unanimous sense of this convention that the attempt to abandon entirely the use of all means of personal restraint is not sanctioned by the true interests of the insane."[25]

This paternalistic justification of psychiatric coercion has remained a prominent theme in psychiatry, not only in America but throughout the civilized world. In 1967—123 years after the drafting of its first resolution—the American Psychiatric Association reaffirmed its support of psychiatric coercion and restraint. In a "Position Statement on the Question of the Adequacy of Treatment," the association declared that "restraints may be imposed [on the patient] from within by pharmacologic means or by locking the door of a ward. Either imposition may be a legitimate component of a treatment program." [26] In the same document, the APA declared that, "It would be manifestly 'poor treatment' to release a patient to commit an unlawful act." [27] Since "unlawful" is in no way qualified, this recommendation endorses involuntary mental hospitalization as a legitimate means of restraining a person from, say, running a red light or cheating on his income tax.

Not only does the MHLP cite approvingly the APA, which endorses psychiatric coercion, but it rests its entire legal strategy on Donaldson's behalf squarely on wrenching the nature and propriety of Donaldson's treatment out of the context in which it actually occurred. In my judgment, such a strategy, especially in the hands of persons ostensibly concerned with civil liberties, is unexcusable. Why? Because in a legal system such as ours, the legitimacy of treatment cannot depend on its efficacy; instead, it must depend on its being undertaken with the informed consent of the patient. This is the principle governing regular medical and surgical treatment. The entire tradition of medical tort litigation supports this principle—that is, the patient's right to request or reject treatment. With the exception of certain life-saving measures imposed on unconscious patients, a medical intervention imposed on a person without his consent is not treatment but assault and battery. The excellent quality of the treatment is no defense. By analogy, it does not matter whether involuntarily committed mental patients receive good, bad, or indifferent treatment or no treatment at all. The very context in which psychiatric

48

interventions are imposed on them renders it impermissible to call such measures treatments. The commission of such an intervention constitutes assault and battery, whereas its omission is simply the absence or omission of assault and battery.*

Finally—in a display of hypocrisy that would be difficult to top—the United States itself appeared as *amicus curiae* on behalf of the committed mental patient! Are we expected to forget—or, better still, to be ignorant of the fact—that the United States had incarcerated Ezra Pound, one of its most famous poets, in the madhouse and kept him there for fourteen years? [28] That a much-admired liberal attorney general of the United States engineered the psychiatric commitment of General Edwin Walker? [30] And that the United States locks up, in its own mental hospital in Washington, D. C., visitors to the White House deemed to be behaving strangely? [31] ** Truly,

---

* Because the Fifth Circuit's right to treatment ruling is likely to result in an increase in psychiatric assaults and batteries, it is ironic that it is precisely such psychiatric coercions that Donaldson, through the MHLP, is now implicitly endorsing. As Schwartz noted, "By holding Donaldson's attending physicians liable for failure to treat him, it [is] likely that mental hospitals, in order not to be liable for not providing treatment, will in the future force such modes of treatment as tranquilizers and ECT upon patients who, as Donaldson did, refuse them."[28]

** To appreciate the role of the United States in the controversy over the right to treatment, we must ponder the following two positions it has recently taken. In January 1975 in a submission to the Supreme Court Solicitor General Robert H. Bork asserted that the government supported the legal position that a patient such as Donaldson enjoyed a "constitutional right to receive such individual treatment as will give him a reasonable opportunity to be cured or to improve his mental condition."[32]

In the summer of 1975, in a brief opposing a suit by the American Association of Physicians and Surgeons (AAPS) asking the Supreme Court to declare the Professional Standards Review Or-with *amici curiae* like these, the Supreme Court needs some *inimici curiae*.

As the pleading on behalf of Donaldson is developed, it becomes, in effect, an ever more powerful defense of civil commitment. Addressing the court directly, the MHLP urges that "in order to affirm the holding of the Court of Appeals, this Court need not decide":

> 1. Whether an involuntarily confined mental patient who is dangerous, either to self or to others, has a right to be treated or be released;
> 2. Whether civil commitment of the mentally ill for any purpose other than treatment is constitutionally permissible.[35]

Why is the MHLP worried that the Supreme Court might rule that civil commitment "for any purpose other than treatment is constitutionally permissible"? I think it would be a good thing if it did so rule: Like any opponent who stands for the wrong thing, it could then more easily be knocked down. As I pointed out earlier, the best justification is no justification.[36] So long as the Supreme Court does not justify commitment at all, it is difficult, legally, to attack its stand on it. (It is, of course, easy enough to attack it intellectually and morally.)

Ironically, the evidence the MHLP cites in connection with the lack of treatment given to Donaldson supports

---

ganizations (PSROs) unconstitutional, the same solicitor general, representing the same United States, declared that "patients whose medical care is provided by public funds have no constitutional right to . . . obtain that care from a physician of their choice."[33]

It is clear that if the United States supports anything, it is the right to treat, not the right to treatment.[34]

not the claim to a right to treatment but its antithesis—namely, that involuntary mental treatment usually harms rather than helps the subject. After remarking on the "deterioration of patients' intellectual, social, and physical functioning as a result of custodial confinement in large understaffed and overcrowded mental hospitals," the authors of the MHLP observe:

One of respondent's expert witnesses, Dr. Walter Fox, testified that respondent's lack of deterioration showed that respondent was uniquely independent: ". . . Mr. Donaldson had . . . more . . . internal strength than most of the people that would find themselves in that sort of total institution for that period of time." [37]

What inference may one draw from Donaldson's ability to maintain his mental functions despite long confinement? One is that he had "more internal strength than most people," a glamorization of Donaldson inconsistent with what we know about him. An inference more consistent with the facts would be that although being locked up in a mental hospital is bad, it is even worse to be locked up in one *and* to receive psychiatric treatment. In my opinion, the doctors at the Florida State Hospital helped Donaldson by not treating him. That Donaldson was not given electroshock or drugs, two treatments he specifically rejected and yet specifically mentioned as being withheld; and that he was allowed to exercise his skills as a defender of his own rights and of the rights of other patients by writing legal briefs—these circumstances suggest that he was treated rather better and more humanely than most patients in most hospitals under similar circumstances.*

What is perhaps most unfortunate about the MHLP's plea for Donaldson is that in its effort to win the case for the right to treatment, the MHLP stoops so low as to falsify the historical record of psychiatry. In promoting the idea of the right to treatment, its advocates must confront the fact that historically mental confinement has had nothing to do with treatment. This fact was adduced in defense of O'Connor. The authors of the MHLP brief brazenly call this claim incorrect: "Petitioner incorrectly asserts that 'the historical basis for the existence of state

---

* In his autobiography, Donaldson himself furnishes evidence to support this view and especially the impression that, at least initially, the doctors at the Florida State Hospital were quite conscientious in caring for him. By "caring" I here mean, of course, that they tried to treat him as good psychiatrists were then supposed to treat their psychotic patients. On February 12, 1957—that is, a month after admission—Dr. J. T. Benbow, the clinical director of the hospital, wrote to Mrs. William Donaldson, explaining that "Mr. Kenneth Donaldson . . . is adjusting quite well to our hospital routine. . . . We do feel that he is quite ill from a mental point of view, however, and we have received some reports of his previous hospitalization suggesting that his illness is of quite long standing."[38] Dr. Benbow concluded the letter by stating that Kenneth Donaldson needed "electroconvulsive treatments," and he enclosed a permission form for Donaldson's parents' signature. Donaldson reproduces this permission form, dated February 19, 1957, signed by William T. Donaldson and witnessed by Marjorie K. Donaldson.[39] Surely, the fact that despite this permission, physicians at the Florida State Hospital refrained from giving Donaldson electroshock treatment must be counted as quite exceptional compassion and decency on their part. Randle McMurphy, in Ken Kesey's fine novel, *One Flew Over the Cuckoo's Nest*,[40] was treated with considerably less compassion but in a manner that presumably fully satisfies the MHLP's claims for a right to treatment.

mental institutions was to safeguard the individual and society, and to relieve the family of the financial and physical burden of caring for the mentally ill.' " [41] The historical record of institutional psychiatry speaks for itself. It is a moving tale of medical crimes, and as such it is one of the most important weapons in the flight for freedom from psychiatric coercion.[42] In defending Donaldson, his legal champions threw away this weapon. It is enough to make one wonder whose side they were on.

In the last analysis, then, I consider the MHLP's claims —ostensibly on behalf of Donaldson but actually on behalf of its own ideas for mental health reform—repugnant because they purvey paternalism in the guise of professionalism, and substitute condescension for respect. The public-interest psychiatrists assume the role of "doctor knows best"; the public-interest lawyers, that of "attorney knows best." The psychiatrists confine and treat their patients as they, the doctors, deem fit, claiming that if the patients only knew psychiatry, the help they are getting is exactly what they would be seeking. Similarly, the lawyers litigate by claiming that their clients are psychotic and in need of involuntary treatment, claiming that if they, the clients, only understood the law, the legal help they are getting is just what they would be seeking. The fact that in some particular cases commitment might help the patient, and the contrived legal strategy of a right to treatment might help the client, only further complicates this matter. Surely, a person who claims that he is well and therefore wants no medical treatment is not treated with respect if psychiatrists act as if he were mentally ill and lawyers as if he had a right to treatment. In the morally murky waters of legal psychiatry, those who strive for freedom

'atric coercion cannot afford to use immoral
. achieving their aims.

V

It may be objected that in view of the practical exigencies of institutional psychiatry, efforts to improve the system are important and legitimate. I do not deny this. But the question is: Do such activities properly fall into the sphere of the ACLU or of any group or individual claiming to be protecting civil liberties? After all, there has never been a shortage of individuals and groups that have tried to improve institutional psychiatry. The ACLU is simply not needed for this task. In my opinion, the real task of civil libertarians concerned with involuntary psychiatry is not how to diminish its abuses, but how to destroy its professional pretensions and its political support. In short, our aim should be not to prettify plantations but to abolish slavery.

Of course, if we cannot eliminate injustice—which is often the case—it is desirable and proper that we help its victims as best we can. However, it is one thing for people to do so as individuals and quite another for them to do so as members of an organization. The appropriate institutions for extending help to needy persons regardless of the circumstances are organizations such as the Red Cross, the Salvation Army, the Rescue Mission, and other charitable agencies. The catch is that it is often difficult for groups—especially for prestigious groups with a high degree of public visibility—to try to improve situation X without thereby authenticating and strengthening the intellectual and moral basis for the existence of situation X. This was the case with slavery and with

Japanese-American relocation camps in the past; and it is the case now with involuntary psychiatry. Perhaps it is sometimes possible to reform these institutionalized injustices without legitimizing them, but this surely requires that those who pursue such a course make their unshakable determination to destroy the system as a moral wrong crystal clear. Since the ACLU has done nothing of the sort with respect to involuntary mental hospitalization, and since, on the contrary, it has always supported, and still supports, commitment laws, the logic of its own behavior drives one inexorably to the conclusion that the ACLU approves of psychiatric slavery and opposes all genuine efforts to abolish it.

The same considerations apply to the MHLP. The evidence I have cited compels one to conclude that the real aim of this organization is not to combat psychiatric coercion but to regulate it. This conclusion is supported by its own bylaws, which state:

In furtherance of its objects and purposes, the Corporation [the MHLP] . . . shall:

1. Identify and implement the rights of the mentally impaired through test case litigation;
2. Work with other organizations in the field of mental health;
3. Conduct a program of clinical education and assist in the training of lawyers and others concerned with mental health law.[43]

Each of these goals is inconsistent with the aim of restoring persons accused of mental illness to full citizenship.

The first goal implies that the mentally impaired have, and ought to have, different rights from those of the rest of the population. Otherwise, there would be nothing to identify or implement. The second goal places the MHLP squarely in opposition to the involuntary mental patient. It is precisely because of other organizations in the mental health field that mental patients are deprived of essential dignities and liberties. If the MHLP wanted to restore the rights of mental patients, it would have to work not *with* but *against* organizations in the mental health field, every one of which supports involuntary psychiatric interventions. The third goal indicates that the MHLP subscribes to the deceptive medical jargon of institutional psychiatry and to the pseudo-therapeutic imagery it fosters. There is nothing clinical about psychiatric prisons and imprisonment. To view loss of liberty under psychiatric auspices from a clinical perspective is to authenticate it.

Although in some of their private comments some of the leaders of the MHLP claim that they oppose involuntary psychiatry, this opposition is in no way reflected in the MHLP's position statements and publications. Specifically, on the issue of involuntary mental hospitalization, the MHLP is on record as implicitly supporting such incarceration by proclaiming that one of the "important rights of the mentally handicapped," is "due process procedures in civil commitment." [44]

Furthermore, the MHLP claims that voluntary mental patients have a right to "adequate treatment"—whatever that is.[45] Worse, still, the project concurs with, and thus legitimizes, the traditional psychiatric policy of treating voluntary patients who want to terminate their psychiatric contacts as involuntary patients—long enough, at least, to allow relatives, psychiatrists, and the courts to change such patients' status from voluntary to involuntary:

> Finally, all voluntary mental health services clients would have the right to withdraw from care or treatment at any time. The only condition placed on this right of immediate termination of care and treatment is that, for purposes of orderly administration, the right of clients in inpatient care and supervised residences is couched in terms of the right to discharge "within the four ordinary business hours following" an oral or written request for release.[46]

Since the MHLP's draft on "Procedures for Voluntary Treatment" is silent about the institutional psychiatrists' right to commit voluntary mental hospital patients who seek release, one is compelled to conclude that the project is not opposed to such a crass betrayal of the patient's trust in his supposedly voluntary status.

VI

I submit that through its brief to the Supreme Court and, more specifically, through its claim that Donaldson had a right to psychiatric treatment while confined in the Florida State Hospital, the MHLP has harmed rather than helped its client. I say this because there are, basically, only three things a lawyer can do for a client victimized by institutional psychiatry. First, he can secure his freedom. Since Donaldson was released before he filed his suit against O'Connor and Gumanis, he already had his freedom. Second, he can sue and try to win money damages for his client. Donaldson's lawyers tried to do this but, perhaps largely because of their tactic, probably will fail. Third, he can dramatize his client's plight as the suffering of the noble soul, a martyr to a cause, the victim of a social evil. It is here, in my opinion, that the MHLP failed, and indeed betrayed, Donaldson.

By claiming that Donaldson had a constitutional right to treatment while in the Florida State Hospital, the attorneys for the MHLP harmed their client by depriving him of his good name, his credibility, his sincerity, his religion, and his sanity. For if Donaldson's own lawyers believe that he had a right to psychiatric treatment while in the hospital, it follows that they themselves must believe that Donaldson was mentally ill while he was incarcerated. If they believe that he had a right to treatment despite his own refusal of treatment, then it follows that they themselves must believe that Donaldson was so mentally incompetent while in the hospital as not to know his own best interests. Finally, if they believe that he had a right to treatment despite his avowed adherence to the faith of Christian Science, then it follows that they themselves must believe that Donaldson's religious affiliation is a sham. With friends like these, Donaldson needs no enemies.

4

The Brief for O'Connor

I

During much of the time that Kenneth Donaldson was confined at the Florida State Hospital, the superintendent of that institution was Dr. J. B. O'Connor. It was O'Connor and John Gumanis, the so-called "treating physician" whom Donaldson sued, who were ordered to pay $38,500 to Donaldson in damages. O'Connor, represented by the attorney general of the State of Florida and two assistant attorneys general, appealed the decision to the Supreme Court. Let us see how O'Connor and his legal champions saw and presented their case.

The brief for O'Connor begins with a résumé of the facts surrounding Donaldson's commitment: "The commitment order states his [Donaldson's] incompetency was due to paranoid schizophrenia with auditory and visual hallucinations and delusions. The order further stated that Donaldson . . . required restraint to prevent self-injury or violence to others. Two physicians served as the investigating commitee for the proceedings."[1]

It is important to note that these judgments about Donaldson's dangerousness were not O'Connor's but those of the court that committed him. Donaldson's dangerousness is thus very much in the record. Nevertheless, Donaldson's legal champions have consistently maintained that there was no evidence of his dangerousness, and the courts have concurred with this judgment.[2] Obviously, I am not asserting that Donaldson was, in fact, dangerous. I am asserting only that there was bureaucratic, legal, and psychiatric evidence that he was dangerous, and that, in view of this evidence it is unreasonable to charge O'Connor, as the brief for Donaldson does, with knowing that Donaldson was not dangerous.[3]

Furthermore, the brief for O'Connor notes something which the brief for Donaldson conveniently omits, namely that Donaldson had been in a mental hospital once before. It also cites another item pertinent to the question of Donaldson's dangerousness: "In January 1957, at the time of his admission to the Florida State Hospital, Donaldson was examined by a Dr. Clark Adair. The examination revealed that Donaldson expressed delusions of persecution for which he blamed 'rich Republicans' and believed that the 'Foreign Policy Association' had attempted to poison him by placing chemicals in his food."[5]

If one accepts the basic medical and moral premises of

traditional psychiatry—which Donaldson's legal champions themselves accept—then it is impossible to maintain that Donaldson was never dangerous. I need not belabor here that I reject this whole psychiatric rhetoric as so much humbug. In my opinion, Donaldson had no constitutional right to treatment, but he most certainly had a constitutional right to his delusions. By insisting that Donaldson had a right to treatment, his legal champions agree to playing in their adversaries' ballpark. They thus commit themselves to the view that institutional psychiatrists are bona fide doctors who diagnose and treat their patients; that they have a right to call persons "patients" even though they do not want to be patients; and that they have a right to diagnose such involuntary patients as dangerous. The upshot is that all the parties to this dispute accept the legitimacy of O'Connor and his staff diagnosing Donaldson as schizophrenic, and even of the claim that they owed him an obligation to treat his schizophrenia; but some of them—that is, the attorneys for the MHLP— reject the accuracy of a part of this diagnosis—namely, that Donaldson was dangerous. This argument for Donaldson simply makes no sense, as it arbitrarily accepts O'Connor's medical authority insofar as it authenticates the basis for Donaldson's claim to a right to treatment—that is, his mental illness; and rejects it insofar as it supports O'Connor's claim to confine Donaldson—that is, his dangerousness.

However, inasmuch as none of these claims and contentions can be empirically verified, it is imperative that we ask not whether Donaldson was mentally ill or dangerous, but rather who has the moral right to make such judgments, and who has the legal authority to impose them on others?

II

According to "scientific" psychiatry and the modern societies that support it, institutional psychiatrists have the above-mentioned rights and powers vis-à-vis their involuntary patients. Donaldson's legal champions have never challenged these psychiatric privileges and powers. Instead, they have tried to sidestep the problems they pose, with the result that the "facts" presented in the briefs for O'Connor and for Donaldson read as if they described two different cases. The MHLP's brief, as I have shown, extolls Donaldson's peacefulness and nondangerousness, whereas the brief for O'Connor sets forth, in the best tradition of institutional psychiatry, the "proofs" of Donaldson's dangerousness. A typical item states: "During January 1964, a meeting of nine members of the staff recommended continued hospitalization. The written opinion of the staff, issued following the meeting with Donaldson, found him dangerous to others and recommended further hospitalization." [6]

Donaldson did not take this lying down. He complained to the state legislature, which led to a further authentication of his dangerousness.* At the instigation of a member of the Florida state legislature, Dr. Franklin J. Calhoun, an independent psychiatrist, examined Donaldson and rendered this opinion: "The results of my examination were in complete accord with the diagnostic evaluation of the hospital staff. . . . I still feel very strongly that Mr. Donaldson is ill, dangerous to society, and should remain hospitalized."[7]

Between 1964 and 1968 Donaldson's repeated requests

---

* All these "facts" are omitted from the MHLP's brief for Donaldson.

62

for release were denied "due to the opinion of the staff that Donaldson was dangerous to himself and others. . . ."[8] To be sure, mental hospital superintendents hide their personal decisions behind such staff decisions, but that is the game of institutional psychiatry. So long as the courts recognize that game as medicine and the implementation of professional standards, it is difficult to understand how they can hold an individual psychiatrist responsible for failing to discharge a non-dangerous patient when that psychiatrist's whole staff has declared that the patient in question was dangerous! Indeed, if a hospital superintendent discharged such a patient, and if that patient committed suicide or a crime, the physician could then be charged with not exercising proper professional care in discharging a dangerous patient—indeed, in discharging him in the face of such an adverse opinion by his own staff. Given these legal realities, how could O'Connor possibly have discharged Donaldson? The two were united by the invisible, but virtually unbreakable, bonds of psychiatric matrimony.[9]

The brief for O'Connor seeks to exonerate him by placing the blame for Donaldson's confinement on the courts. In this case, this classic psychiatric evasion of responsibility is supported by unusually good evidence. Donaldson was diagnosed as a dangerous paranoid schizophrenic; he refused treatment; and the propriety of his confinement in the hospital was legitimized by the courts at least fifteen times.[10]

III

The brief for O'Connor concludes with an appeal to the Supreme Court to reverse the lower courts' decision because, first, the doctrine of a right to treatment cannot be defined or implemented; second, Donaldson refused the treatments he had been offered; and third, even if a constitutional right to treatment were now promulgated, none existed when Donaldson was hospitalized, and it would be unjust to apply it to O'Connor retroactively.

The roles are now completely reversed. Donaldson, the institutionalized psychotic, says he has a right to treatment. O'Connor, the institutional psychiatrist, counters, citing my argument, that there can be no such right:

> Dr. Szasz believes that what is termed a "right" to treatment should be labeled a "claim" for treatment and points out that a "right" to treatment for patients would seriously impair a physician's prerogatives of choosing his patients and methods of treatment. This conflict is heightened in a state mental hospital where a physician cannot choose his patients.[11]

O'Connor's claims are clearly more consistent with the facts than Donaldson's. O'Connor never wanted Donaldson as a patient. He accepted him because the courts said he must. Had the courts also ordered O'Connor to give Donaldson this or that specific treatment, no doubt O'Connor would have carried out that order too. He was evidently a loyal state hospital physician, working for those who hired him, paid him, and had the legal authority to define his rights and duties. Not so Donaldson, who claimed he did not want to be a mental hospital patient but managed to get himself hospitalized twice; and who claimed he did not want any psychiatric treatment but sued for a deprivation of his "right to treatment."

Responding to this glaring inconsistency in Donaldson's position, the brief for O'Connor argues that "even assuming the existence of a right to treatment, Donaldson could not present a valid claim. He failed to uphold his corresponding duty to be treated. His actions should have been construed as an effective waiver or repudiation of any right to treatment."[12]

O'Connor's brief tries to remind the court of the real nature and function of state mental hospitals. Here again one faces the boundless irony of this case—Donaldson pleading, implicitly, that we reaffirm and strengthen all that is coercive and corrupt in institutional psychiatry; and O'Connor pleading, explicitly, that we face the facts about it and confront their moral and practical implications. "State mental hospitals," observes the O'Connor brief, "are a creature and occasional victim of legislative fiat. . . . The administrator and staff have no meaningful control over the facilities and resources at their disposal. Likewise, they must accept every patient sent to them under a valid commitment order."[13]

The inexorable consequences of a collectivized, state-operated psychiatry are here, at least, frankly acknowledged. In such a system, both patient and psychiatrist are constrained: the former is much like a prisoner and the latter much like his jailer, the two locked into a mutual embrace by the legislatures and the courts. All this has been concealed by the rhetoric of traditional psychiatry, pontificating about diagnoses, hospitals, and doctors. It is now concealed still further by the rhetoric of the promoters of the doctrine of the right to treatment, pontificating about the Constitution, mental illness, and treatment.

5

The Brief
for the American
Psychiatric Association

I

After the *Donaldson* case was appealed to the Supreme Court, the American Psychiatric Association (APA) filed an *amicus curiae* brief with the consent of both parties. The brief reveals, first of all, that like virtually everything in institutional psychiatry, this document is misleadingly titled. The APA here speaks not as a friend of the court but as a friend of itself. Introducing the brief in the *American Journal of Psychiatry*, Alan A. Stone, Chairman of the APA Commission on Judicial Action, writes:

66

The amicus curiae brief of the American Psychiatric Association is published here both to emphasize a momentous historical event in psychiatry and to share with the membership the substantive thinking that went into APA participation. . . . The Supreme Court has agreed to accept the case; this marks the first time in the history of the United States that its highest tribunal has considered the rights of the non-criminally mentally ill. It will also be the first instance that the court will be considering the rights and duties of the psychiatrists who attend those patients. The APA brief asks the court to do justice to both patients and physicians.[1]

This statement illustrates many of the points I have made concerning the language of institutional psychiatry and the justification of involuntary psychiatric interventions. Nowhere in this paragraph is there any reference to the fact that the *Donaldson* case concerns a man who was an involuntary patient. And the institutional psychiatrists are called simply "physicians." If they were really just physicians, like dermatologists or gynecologists, there would be no need for a special judicial determination of their rights and duties. In fact, institutional psychiatrists are, in the court's own words, "agent[s] of the State."[2] That is why their rights and duties vis-à-vis patients are so problematic.

Moreover, Stone's and the APA's claim that the "brief asks the court to do justice to both patients and physicians" is flatly contradicted by the language of the association's own biweekly newspaper. On October 16, 1974 *Psychiatric News* reported the APA's intention to file an *amicus curiae* brief in the Donaldson case. The front-page story was headlined: "APA Enters Florida Case to Defend Psychiatrists."[3] According to this story, the APA was squarely against Donaldson and the courts that awarded him damages from O'Connor and Gumanis, mainly on the grounds that the courts had validated Donaldson's confinement fifteen separate times.[4]

Stone's introduction to the APA's *amicus curiae* brief requires one more comment. The *Donaldson* case, he writes, concerns "the rights of the noncriminally mentally ill."[5] I maintain that the very act of speaking of the rights of the non-criminally mentally ill precludes one from raising the really important questions concerning the *Donaldson* case, such as: How is a person transformed from a normal American citizen into a non-criminal mentally ill individual? How can that person object to or resist this transformation, and who has the right to initiate it and carry it through to completion? The language of the APA effectively eludes these crucial questions. Its plea for justice is nothing less than a request for permission to transform people from persons to patients unhindered by legislative or judicial restraints. American psychiatrists have, after all, always favored "simple, medical criteria for commitment."[6]

II

The APA's brief is, more than anything else, a massive linguistic concealment and justification of psychiatric wardens as doctors, psychiatric prisons as hospitals, psychiatric stigmatizations as diagnoses, and involuntary psychiatric interventions as medical treatments. To appreciate this point, the brief must be read carefully in its entirety. In its very first sentence, the brief implies that institu-

68

tional psychiatrists function vis-à-vis their captive clients as doctors of medicine.[7] This is an untruth, not because these psychiatrists are necessarily bad men and women, but because they function vis-à-vis their patients as agents of the state.* The hospitals they work in are called, in the main, "state hospitals." Wherever they might work, they are authorized by the state to detain and treat persons against their will. It is for the rights of these doctors, who are the executors of the will of the people through their lawmakers—as against the rights of doctors who are the executors of the will of their patients through the patients' consent to treatment—that the APA is pleading in its brief of *amicus curiae:*

> Amicus believes this case to be of historic importance to the future of mental health care in the nation's public mental institutions. . . . The opinion below decides two questions that are fundamental to the future course of mental health care in this country. First, does the involuntarily committed patient at a state mental institution have a constitutional right to a level of treatment reasonably calculated to improve his or her mental condition? . . . The court below answered the first question by holding that there *is* a constitutional right to an adequate level of treatment, and that Respondent Kenneth Donaldson did not receive this level of care. Amicus APA whole-

* The unanimous opinion of the Court in the *Donaldson* case acknowledges this.[8] This, in turn, raises the question of whether O'Connor was supposed to be an agent-doctor or agent-warden? Since he had the power to confine and to release from confinement, he was clearly an agent-warden. This makes Donaldson a prisoner, an inference the justices seemed unwilling to draw from their own premises.

heartedly supports the Court of Appeals decision on this issue.[9]

Evidently the APA likes the idea that psychiatrists should have *not only* a right to imprison innocent individuals in insane asylums *but also* a right to impose any kind of intervention on them accredited as "treatment" by themselves and the courts. Whether we think this is good or bad, let us at least be honest enough to call it by its proper name: It is not a right to treatment but a right to treat.[10] In general, involuntary mental patients do not want the treatment they get from institutional psychiatrists. If they did, they would not have to be incarcerated and coerced, legally and personally, into submitting to the interventions which the psychiatrists call treatment, but the patients consider torture.

Ironically, institutional psychiatrists already have a right to treat, especially if their patients are declared incompetent. If so, why do they clamor for some sort of legal articulation of this right? The demand for the right to treatment is actually a cover for the demand for more funds to expand psychiatric facilities, personnel, and power. The APA itself acknowledges this: "Indeed, such actions [for damages against the responsible state agency] may be the most effective method to loosen the legislature's pursestrings, so that sufficient resources do become available."[11]

III

In effect, the APA position is that psychiatrists are doctors, doctors treat patients, and hence what psychiatrists do is a good thing. If something bad happens, it must be someone else's fault. Whose? The responsible state agency's. The culprits are those who are too niggardly with the public funds and do not provide enough psychiatrists and good hospitals to properly implement the right to treatment. The APA articulates the problem, and its proper solution, as follows:

> [The second question is], assuming there is such a right [to treatment], who should be responsible for providing the remedy when an institution has inadequate resources to provide that level of treatment? . . . Regarding [this] second major question—the proper remedy for violation of this new right—Amicus believes the court below committed a serious error.[12]

In other words, the APA maintains that the psychiatrist, as doctor, has an obligation to satisfy the patient's right to treatment. However, if the patient is denied this right, the doctor, as state official, should not be held responsible for such a denial. The Court of Appeals ruling "conflicts with numerous decisions from other courts holding that state officials are not liable personally for damages when in good faith they have been unable to comply with a newly declared constitutional right."[13] The APA's war of words against its opponents could not be clearer. When it promotes treatment for involuntary patients, it calls wardens "doctors"; when it promotes individual nonresponsibility for malpractice, it calls doctors "state officials."

It is, of course, impossible here to review and analyze sentence by sentence and word by word, the APA's brief, although doing so would reveal that what organized psychiatry now wants is what it has always wanted: more power, more public funds, and less legal accountability. To support this contention, I shall cite a few more passages from the APA's *amicus sui brief*. Pleading with the court to "affirm the constitutional right to treatment," the association acknowledges that: "The present case starkly reveals the overwhelming shame and challenge of the nation's mental health care system. The deplorable conditions shown to exist at Florida State Hospital at Chattahoochee are all too common in many jurisdictions throughout the country."[14]

There is no mental health care system in this or any other nation. There are only psychiatric prisons. Furthermore, this case has not revealed anything that has not been perfectly obvious for the past three hundred years. The APA's seeming admission of deplorable conditions in mental hospitals is patently insincere and self-serving. "Meaningful psychiatric care was not, and cannot be, provided under such circumstances," the brief proclaims in a statement with which I wholeheartedly agree.[15] But what would follow from such a state of affairs, were it taken seriously? In a hospital without adequate facilities for open heart surgery, the doctors do not accept patients requiring such surgery. *Mutatis mutandis*, in a hospital without adequate facilities for meaningful psychiatric care, the doctors should not accept patients who require such care. Hence, the first thing the APA ought to do is to lobby for the suspension of all admissions to hospitals that lack adequate facilities. Instead, it is lobbying for the right to treat patients who do not even want treatment, while loudly bewailing that the system prevents doctors from providing it.

IV

The Donaldson affair is, from beginning to end, a morally repugnant tragi-comedy. Donaldson claims never to have been ill and yet sues for damages on the grounds that he was deprived of his constitutional right to treatment. The APA claims that no one can be treated in institutions like the Florida State Hospital but that the psychiatrists who admitted, confined, and non-treated Donaldson are nevertheless totally blameless for this "unspeakable tragedy":

> It is an unspeakable tragedy when a mentally ill person is crowded into a facility like Chattahoochee, given little or no medical treatment, and allowed to remain there for years on end. Amicus believes strongly that such conditions violate the patient's constitutional right to treatment. The responsibility for a remedy, however, must lie with those who have the power to correct these conditions.[16]

This is a pitiful argument. If a patient were to offer it, psychiatrists would call him a psychopath. If the system is as bad as it is here stated to be—and it actually is much worse—then psychiatrists could easily remedy it by concerted action. They could quit working with committed patients. If psychiatrists would simply not commit or admit patients to hospitals that, according to the APA itself, are non-therapeutic or anti-therapeutic, then these tragic conditions soon would disappear. No one is compelled to be a psychiatrist; and even if he is a psychiatrist, he need not be a psychiatric slave master.

A comparison of involuntary servitude and involuntary

psychiatry makes one realize that in at least one respect the practical situation of those who wanted to abolish chattel slavery was more favorable than is the practical situation of those who want to abolish psychiatric slavery. Slavery was recognized as a condition inflicted by one person on another. The slaveholders could therefore never evade the responsibility for having slaves and for the condition of slavery. They could not credibly claim that blackness was some sort of mysterious disease for which slavery was the cure—although Benjamin Rush insisted that Negritude was a form of congenital leprosy,[17] and Samuel Cartwright maintained that Negro slaves escaped to the free states not because they preferred liberty to servitude but because they suffered from "drapetomania," a mental illness that made them run away.[18]

Unlike the slaveholders, institutional psychiatrists can, and do, avoid responsibility for the condition of psychiatric slavery by attributing it to, and confusing it with, the condition of mental illness. According to this official psychiatric view, the mental patient is indeed a victim—but he is a victim not of institutional psychiatry but of mental illness. This evasion of moral responsibility for psychiatric slavery, which pervades the psychiatric literature on involuntary psychiatric interventions, surfaces in this typical phrase in the APA's brief: "Amicus believes that such [mental hospital] conditions violate the patient's constitutional right to treatment."[19] However, conditions, in the abstract, cannot violate anyone's rights. Only persons can—even if they do so through institutions that formally legitimize such victimizations rather than through individual initiative. Involuntary mental patients are clearly victimized. It is past time that we clearly identified their victimizers.

I submit that the plight of the so-called mental patient will not be clearly seen, and hence will not be effectively remedied, until the APA is recognized as not only an organization of doctors, but also a lobby for psychiatric slavery. Psychiatrists and jurists have created this tragedy together and, like thieves falling out among themselves, each is now trying to pin the blame for it on the other. This is a good omen in that it heralds the disintegration of psychiatric slavery.

This disintegration could perhaps be hastened if we acknowledged the full horror of psychiatric slavery and recognized it for the historical, rather than personal, wrong that it is. For historical wrongs there can be no personal reckoning, no personal punishments. What there can be—and must be, if the wrong is to be righted—is a decisive moral recognition of the wrong and an abolition of the economic, legal, and political authentications and supports for its perpetuation. In collective life, as in personal life, the best way to repent for a wrong is by not repeating it.

6

The Supreme Court's Decision in *O'Connor v. Donaldson*

I

When the Fifth Circuit Court of Appeals upheld the award of money damages to Donaldson, the psychiatrists appealed to the United States Supreme Court. Donaldson claimed that by confinement without treatment, O'Connor had unconstitutionally deprived him of his liberty.[1] O'Connor argued in defense that he had acted in good faith, since "state law, which he believed valid, had authorized indefinite custodial confinement of the 'sick,' even if they were not treated."[2]

How did the Supreme Court resolve this conflict? Technically, by upholding Donaldson. Actually, by upholding O'Connor. The court vacated the money damages awarded Donaldson which, after all, was the only recompense that he had received for all his troubles. The court's formally unanimous opinion thus betrays a bottomless ambivalence toward the issues this case presents, and large areas of un-resolved—perhaps even unarticulated—differences among the justices. My own conjecture is that the court had agreed to hear this case believing that it offered a good platform for articulating some sort of "right to treatment" for mental patients. It discovered, perhaps too late for comfort, that there was more to this problem than met the eye, and then the court sidestepped the basic issues by deciding the case so narrowly that its ruling amounted essentially to no decision at all. A careful reading of the court's opinion is consistent with these interpretations. Summarizing the case, the Supreme Court noted that the Court of Appeals declared that,

[R]egardless of the grounds for involuntary civil commitment, a person confined against his will at a state mental institution has a "constitutional right to receive such individual treatment as will give him a reasonable opportunity to be cured or to improve his mental condition." Conversely, the court's opinion implied that it is constitutionally permissible for a State to confine a mentally ill person against his will in order to treat his illness, regardless of whether his illness renders him dangerous to himself or others.[3]

These are absurd contentions, for reasons I have indicated earlier and elsewhere.[4] Evidently the justices of the Supreme Court thought so also. In any case, they felt it was better not to deal with them, and accordingly redefined the case, as follows:

> We have concluded that the difficult issues of constitutional law dealt with by the Court of Appeals are not presented by this case in its present posture. Specifically, there is no reason now to decide whether mentally ill persons dangerous to themselves or to others have a right to treatment upon compulsory confinement by the State, or whether the State may compulsorily confine a nondangerous, mentally ill individual for the purpose of treatment. As we view it, this case raises a single, relatively simple, but nonetheless important question concerning every man's constitutional right to liberty.[5]

If one stopped right here, one might think the court was about to address itself to the issue of civil commitment. But that, too, was deemed irrelevant to the case:

> We need not decide whether, when, or by what procedures, a mentally ill person may be confined by the State on any of the grounds which, under contemporary statutes, are generally advanced to justify involuntary confinement of such a person—to prevent injury to the public, to ensure his own survival or safety, or to alleviate or cure his illness.[6]

II

What was there left to consider? What have become known in legal-psychiatric jargon as the mental patient's "post-confinement rights." The contention that the Supreme Court fastened on was that O'Connor did not release Donaldson sooner than he did. This was Donaldson's post-confinement right that O'Connor had violated:

> In short, a State cannot constitutionally confine without more [*sic*] a nondangerous individual who is capable of surviving safely in freedom by himself or with the help of willing and responsible family members or friends. Since the jury found, upon ample evidence, that O'Connor, as an agent of the State, knowingly did so confine Donaldson, it properly concluded that O'Connor violated Donaldson's constitutional right to freedom.[7]

Actually, O'Connor did not violate Donaldson's constitutional right to freedom: He took Donaldson in custody in conformity with the regulations of the Florida commitment laws; he held him in custody in conformity with those laws; and he allowed him to file periodic appeals with the courts for release, all of which upheld the legality of his confinement. I would hazard the guess that, on remand, the judgment against O'Connor will be reversed.

There is indeed evidence that the justices were leaning toward the view that O'Connor should not be held liable. They sent the case back to the district court for redetermination of O'Connor's liability, in the light of a standard of immunity specifying that "an official has, of course, no duty to anticipate unforeseeable constitutional developments."[8] It seems to me that the court is here saying two things: First, that O'Connor is legally innocent of any wrongdoing and the judgment against him should be reversed; and second, that in the future institutional psychiatrists ought to be nicer to their institutionalized in-

79

mates. As with slavery before, the justices' hearts went out to the victim, but their minds supported the victimizer.[9] It is difficult to see, given the strictures of the Donaldson case, what else they could have done that would have been much better.

In vacating the judgment of the Court of Appeals and remanding the case, the justices instructed the lower court to consider "whether the District Judge's failure to instruct with regard to the effect of O'Connor's claimed reliance on state law rendered inadequate the instructions as to O'Connor's liability for compensatory and punitive damages."[10] And, in a significant footnote to this statement, they added:

Upon remand, the Court of Appeals is to consider only the question whether O'Connor is to be held liable for monetary damages for violating Donaldson's constitutional right to liberty. . . . Of necessity our decision vacating the judgment of the Court of Appeals deprives that court's opinion of precedential effect, leaving this Court's opinion and judgment as the sole law of the case.[11]

III

One of the most important aspects of this case is the issue of Donaldson's alleged dangerousness. The lower courts ruled that Donaldson was not dangerous, and the Supreme Court based its own decision on an uncritical acceptance of this ruling. But these judicial pronouncements about the psychiatrists' duties toward non-dangerous mental patients "capable of surviving safely in freedom" are utterly meaningless; and the decisions based on them are necessarily toothless.

Indeed, by using the term "dangerousness" casually and uncritically, all the courts ruling on the *Donaldson* case are guilty of authenticating a term crucial in the debate about forensic psychiatry that may be even more misleading than "mental illness" or "treatment." I say this partly because psychiatric dangerousness is undefined and undefinable, and partly because it is premised on a judgment rendered in retrospect. Mental patients released from hospitals as non-dangerous sometimes proceed to injure or kill themselves or others. It is then concluded that they were dangerous all along, and the hospital authorities may be held liable for their release. To the extent that the Donaldson judgment rests on his non-dangerousness, it could be, or could have been, vitiated at any time by Donaldson's committing suicide or engaging in some criminal act—possibilities open to any human being by virtue of his very freedom.

Moreover, by couching their judgments in terms of an unspecified non-dangerousness, the justices of the Supreme Court have effectively bypassed the crucial question that underlies all the controversies of institutional psychiatry, namely: Whose definition of dangerousness will the courts support? A longstanding tacit agreement exists between law and psychiatry which permits the institutional psychiatrist to call people "mentally ill" and "dangerous," and the courts to support or reject these diagnoses. Actually, such psychiatric judgments are usually rubber-stamped by the courts. In any case, it is clear that for judicial purposes the patient's judgment of his own dangerousness is utterly irrelevant. "This ruling," comments Louis Kopolow, Staff Psychiatrist for the Patients' Rights and Advocacy Programs of the National Institute of Mental Health, "does not directly apply to those who *might be* considered dangerous by *a* psychiatrist [or] to those who *might be* dangerous to themselves . . ." (emphasis added).[12] Unfortunately and perhaps unwittingly the justices of the Supreme Court are thus perpetuating the worst intellectual and moral abuses of institutional psychiatry. Where is the institutional psychiatrist who would agree that he is confining non-dangerous persons who could survive safely in freedom? O'Connor never agreed that Donaldson fell into that class; nor could any self-respecting institutional psychiatrist admit that any of his commited patients fall into it. In effect the Supreme Court identified a class of mental patients without any members.

Worse still, the problem of Donaldson's dangerousness is treated as if it were a question of fact rather than a judgment rendered by fallible and corruptible human beings and social institutions—in particular, by psychiatrists, judges, and courts. For fifteen years, courts ruled that Donaldson was dangerous. After he was released, several courts ruled that he is not, and never was, dangerous. This can mean only that the courts imprisoned a "psychiatrically innocent"—that is, non-dangerous—person. It defies all logic to claim that because Donaldson was so imprisoned, he was entitled to treatment while in "prison," or to damages from the "warden" in charge of his prison.

IV

Several aspects of *O'Connor* v. *Donaldson* make it exceptionally troublesome from a legal point of view.

Donaldson was a Christian Scientist. He requested that he be given no shock treatment or drugs, a request his psychiatrists respected. Yet his suit was for money damages from his psychiatrists for confining him without treatment. By refusing to hear the case, the court could have withheld its imprimatur from the lower courts' decision without giving any reasons. To be sure, it would have then, by default, given the Fifth Circuit's right-to-treatment ruling precedential effect which, by hearing the case, the court denied. However, the court would have been more evenhanded if it had refused to grant *certiorari* to both *Donaldson* v. *O'Connor* and *O'Connor* v. *Donaldson.*

Judicially, the abolitionist cause would be best served if the Supreme Court heard the case of a committed mental patient and ruled that his incarceration was unconstitutional, a decision that may well constitute an encroachment on the prerogatives of the legislature. In *Donaldson,* however, the court heard a case premised on the legitimacy of psychiatric slavery. It was thus compelled to reach a decision that was, more or less, pro-slavery. The point is that while the court could have reached a decision that was even more pro-slavery than the one it reached, it could not, given the context of *O'Connor* v. *Donaldson,* reach a decision that was decisively anti-slavery. As one legal commentator has put it: "*Donaldson* is but a first step in the Supreme Court's recognition of the post-commitment constitutional rights of institutionalized persons who have been involuntarily incarcerated *after a constitutionally sound civil commitment proceeding* (emphasis added).[13]

Ironically, many commentators on the *Donaldson* case never tire of emphasizing, with evident satisfaction, that it marks the first time in the history of the United States that the Supreme Court has considered the rights of the noncriminally mentally ill. They fail to see this as dramatic proof of how stubbornly the Supreme Court has refused to face the brutal facts of psychiatric slavery. In its 199-year history, the court has tacitly approved of psychiatric imprisonment as medical hospitalization and of psychiatric torture as medical treatment. The complexities and confusions of the *Donaldson* case are the consequences of this, perhaps the most massive, denial of the very spirit of our national identity since the issue of slavery itself.[14]

V

Let us now consider Chief Justice Burger's separate opinion which, although it received scanty mention in the popular press, seems more important than the unanimous opinion with which it formally concurs but from which it philosophically dissents. Justice Burger emphasizes that Donaldson consistently refused treatment, and that this has greater bearing on O'Connor's alleged liability for nontreatment than it has been given:

The Court appropriately takes notice of the uncertainties of psychiatric diagnosis and therapy, and the reported cases are replete with evidence of the divergence of medical opinion in this vexing area. . . . Nonetheless, one of the few areas of agreement among behavioral specialists is that an uncooperative patient cannot benefit from therapy and that the first step in effective treatment is acknowledgement by the patient that he is suffering from an abnormal condition. . . . Donaldson's adamant refusal to do so

84

should be taken into account in considering petitioner's good-faith defense.[15]

Burger also notes that O'Connor's decision to detain Donaldson could not be considered arbitrary or unreasonable, as it was repeatedly authorized by the courts. One of his writs of habeas corpus had been appealed to the Supreme Court, which denied hearing it only one year before Donaldson was released:

Whatever the reasons for the state courts' repeated denials of relief, and regardless of whether they correctly resolved the issue tendered to them, petitioner and the other members of the medical staff at Florida State Hospital would surely have been justified in considering each such judicial decision as an approval of continued confinement and an independent intervening reason for continuing Donaldson's custody.[16]

Burger then lectures the Court of Appeals, and perhaps his own brethren, on the true history of psychiatry:

In short, the idea that States may not confine the mentally ill except for the purpose of providing them with treatment is of very recent origin, and there is no historical basis for imposing such a limitation on state power. . . . There can be little doubt that in the exercise of its police power a State may confine individuals solely to protect society from the dangers of significant antisocial acts or communicable disease. . . . Additionally, the states are vested with the historic *parens patriae* power. . . . The classic example of this role is when a State undertakes to act as "the general guardian of all infants, idiots, and lunatics."[17]

Given the thus unchallenged constitutional legitimacy of applying traditional principles of *parens patriae* to the mentally ill, it does not follow, asserts Burger, that there need be any limitations on its requiring treatment:

[T]he existence of some due process limitations on the *parens patriae* power does not justify the further conclusion that it may be exercised to confine a mentally ill person only if the purpose of the confinement is treatment. Despite many recent advances in medical knowledge, it remains a stubborn fact that there are many forms of mental illness which are not understood, some which are untreatable in the sense that no effective therapy has yet been discovered for them, and that rates of "cure" are generally low. . . . Similarly, as previously observed, it is universally recognized as fundamental to effective therapy that the patient acknowledge his illness and cooperate with those attempting to give treatment; yet the failure of a large proportion of mentally ill persons to do so is a common phenomenon.[18]

In the course of his "concurring dissent," Burger remarks on the inadequacy of O'Connor's legal defense, especially in not pressing the point that only a year before his release the Supreme Court itself refused to hear one of Donaldson's appeals.[19] It is important to note that in the *Donaldson* case the arguments for the psychiatrist-defendants were every bit as inept as the arguments for

86

the patient were crafty. It is as if, while in the hospital, O'Connor had all the power and Donaldson all the true words about what was happening, whereas once out of the hospital Donaldson had all the power and O'Connor all the true words.*

Justice Burger, it would seem, is the only one among all of the participants in this tragi-comedy who is willing to address himself to psychiatric facts rather than to psychiatric fictions. His analysis of the case is cogent, and his conclusion is compelling:

> In sum, I cannot accept the reasoning of the Court of Appeals and can discern no other basis for equating an involuntarily committed mental patient's unquestioned constitutional right not to be confined without due process of law with a constitutional right to *treatment*. Given the present state of medical knowledge regarding abnormal human behavior and its treatment, few things would be more fraught with peril than to irrevocably condition a State's power to protect the mentally ill upon the providing of "such treatment as will give [them] a realistic opportunity to be cured." Nor can I accept the theory that a State may lawfully confine an individual thought to need treatment and justify that deprivation of liberty

---

* In 1971, Dr. J. B. O'Connor retired as Superintendent of the Florida State Hospital. On November 21, 1975, at the age of sixty-seven, he died. Attorneys for the MHLP thereupon filed a motion to substitute the executor of O'Connor's estate as defendant in Donaldson's action against O'Connor and petitioned the court for summary judgment for their client. Attorneys for O'Connor's estate filed a brief opposing summary judgment. This is how the matter of *O'Connor* v. *Donaldson* stood in June, 1976, when this manuscript went into production.

solely by providing some treatment. Our concepts of due process would not tolerate such a "trade-off." Because the Court of Appeals' analysis could be read as authorizing those results, it should not be followed.[20]

According to the entire court, then, involuntarily hospitalized mental patients do *not* have a constitutional right to treatment.

7

Interpretations of the Supreme Court's *Donaldson* Decision

I

Judging by the interpretations of the *Donaldson* decision in both the popular and professional press, the justices could scarcely have been more successful in being misunderstood. They declared that they need not decide whether a committed mental patient has a right to treatment, nor on what grounds a person may be committed to a mental hospital. Nevertheless, the press uniformly reported that the Supreme Court had ruled that involuntary mental patients have a constitutional right to treatment and that such patients must be either treated or released. A brief review of the extensive press coverage of the *Donaldson* decision will illustrate this astonishing misreading and misreporting of the case.

In a long news story entitled "Historic Mental Health Ruling," the *Washington Post* gave a reasonably accurate account of the issues in the case and the court's resolution of them.[1] But it then interpreted the ruling as a victory for mental patients. One part of the report was subtitled "After nearly 20 years, an ex-mental patient is vindicated."[2] This ignored the facts that Donaldson had been released before he filed his suit against his psychiatrists; that the award itself was contingent on further proceedings; and that the Supreme Court had paid no attention to Donaldson's claim that he had never been ill.

As for the experts canvassed, the *Post* found them all very happy with the decision. Bertram Brown, director of the National Institute of Mental Health, acclaimed the *Donaldson* decision as giving "strong impetus to the movement away from treatment in large institutions which too often become custodial confinement."[3] If so, this would merely transfer involuntary mental patients from psychiatric imprisonment in hospitals to psychiatric parole in clinics. The players and the game remain the same: Psychiatrists retain the power to control people by means of involuntary treatment, and the patients retain the stigma and role of madmen who must submit to their medical masters. Only the location of the compulsory association between institutional psychiatrist and involuntary mental patient changes.

The report of the case in *The New York Times* was inaccurate and misleading. The headline of the story, "High Court Curbs Power to Confine the Mentally Ill," suggested that the court had ruled on commitment, which it had not.[4] For the *Times,* Bruce Ennis had this to say about the meaning of the court's decision "[M]ental hospitals as we have known them can no longer exist in this country as dumping grounds for the old, the poor, and the friendless. [Such institutions] will have to re-evaluate the status of each patient."[5]

Claiming to have triumphed over the evils of institutional psychiatry, the victor here speaks, apparently unaware of what he is saying, in the language of the vanquished. Ennis does not say, as it seems to me he ought to, that being old, poor, or friendless are not diseases, and that such persons are not patients unless they choose to be. Instead, he says that institutional psychiatrists "will have to re-evaluate the status of each patient." But such re-evaluation will only mean that, should institutional psychiatrists choose to retain their victims, they will define them as mentally ill, dangerous, and receiving treatment. And should they choose to reject them and decide to throw them out of the hospital, even if they, the chronic mental patients, want to stay, then they will define them as no longer ill, not dangerous, and fit to be discharged.

Among the authorities interviewed, the *Times* quotes an unnamed spokesman for the New York Civil Liberties Union who called the ruling "a landmark legal victory in the effort to oppose involuntary commitment of mental patients."[6] It is no such thing. The Supreme Court's decision relates only to the "post-commitment rights" of already committed patients. To misunderstand this is to fail to see that what is here being claimed as a victory for mental patients is, instead, another victory for institutional psychiatrists. *

---

* This view is supported by a "Memo from the Director" of the National Institute of Mental Health distributed to psychiatric ad-

II

The reports on the *Donaldson* case in *Time* and *Newsweek* were no better. *Time* headlined its account "Opening the Asylums,"[8] which is not exactly what the court had done. The sensational headline was contradicted in the body of the story, where the reader could learn that, "For all the importance of the *Donaldson* decision, the court conceded that it was merely starting its work on the rigths of mental patients."[9] Although the court conceded no such thing, it is interesting to note that *Time* interprets the court's decision as a reaffirmation of the constitutionality of civil commitment, requiring, perhaps, only more precise criteria for it: "Left to future cases were such matters as . . . what are fair standards for commitment."[10]

The headline in *Newsweek*, "Freeing Mental Patients," was equally inaccurate.[11] The *Newsweek* story also implied that the monetary damage awarded to Donaldson by the lower courts was upheld by the Supreme Court. In addition to these mistakes of fact, *Newsweek* quoted Bruce Ennis, who told the *Washington Post* that "thousands, perhaps even hundreds of thousands of harmless mental patients will eventually be released from confinement because of the [Donaldson] decision,"[12] as stating

---

ministrators throughout the country in December 1975. Concluding his introduction to this memo—consisting of a reprinting of the Supreme Court's *Donaldson* decision and an analysis of its implications—Bertram S. Brown, the Director of NIMH, writes: "Finally, I would like to express my personal conviction that the *Donaldson* decision is an important victory for everyone who believes that the mentally ill should receive treatment and not merely custodial confinement."[7] In short, Brown clearly believes that the ruling strengthens rather than weakens psychiatric slavery.

92

to its own reporter that "No one is talking about the precipitous, wholesale release of thousands of mental patients tomorrow. There must be adequate planning for such discharges."[13] This statement betrays the official civil libertarian's deeply ingrained ambivalence toward so-called mental patients. For if Donaldson was falsely imprisoned in a mental hospital, as Ennis claimed, then he and others in his position deserve that they be restored to liberty immediately—not after adequate planning for it by those who are illegally imprisoning them.

One of the more interesting reactions to the Donaldson decision is a front-page report in the September 1975 issue of *Civil Liberties*, the official organ of the American Civil Liberties Union. Its interpretation of this ruling is remarkable, to say the least. First, the report was entitled "High Court Upholds Donaldson," a headline from which the unwary reader would infer that the Supreme Court upheld the money damages awarded to Donaldson by the lower courts.[14] Second, the ACLU claimed sole proprietary rights in the case, identifying it as "brought by the American Civil Liberties Union," thus slighting both Donaldson's and Birnbaum's efforts.[15] Third, the ACLU laid claims also to the concept of the right to treatment, calling the *Donaldson* ruling, supposedly prohibiting confinement without treatment, "the Union's most important victory since 1973."[16]*

* These claims are an outrageous attempt to falsify the historical record and make the ACLU appear as a long-time champion of the rights of the mentally ill. As I have noted earlier,[17] the ACLU has, in fact, been one of the "public-spirited" organizations responsible for the deprivations of the rights of the mentally ill. Moreover, the ACLU's self-aggrandizing claims about the *Donaldson* case are flatly contradicted by Donaldson in his autobiographical account of his hospitalization.[18] Even Birnbaum, a loyal mem-

This brazen attempt to redefine and recast the ultimate outcome of the *Donaldson* case, from ambiguous victory for O'Connor to absolute victory for Donaldson, is carried through systematically by various spokesmen for the MHLP. In an article arrogantly mistitled "The Supreme Court Unlocks Doors," Paul Friedman, the managing attorney for the MHLP, hails the decision as one whose "significance is great indeed and [whose] ramifications are only beginning to be felt."[20] According to Friedman, "At its most basic level, the opinion says that the members of our highest court care about the plight of the mentally handicapped and recognize that the United States Constitution protects this under-represented minority just as it protects other citizens."[21]

This simply is not true. If the Supreme Court had really cared about Donaldson's plight, it would have heard his appeal for freedom rather than O'Connor's appeal for reversal of the money damages against him. Moreover, Friedman's phrase reveals his profoundly condescending attitude toward so-called mental patients and his tacit assumption that the Supreme Court's attitude toward them is similar. "Caring" is not a part of the court's business. The court need not care about Blacks, Jews, women, or mental patients. Instead, what the Supreme Court must do is to ensure that the lower courts,

---

ber of the ACLU and co-counsel with Ennis in the *Donaldson* case, cannot refrain from pointing out that "the American Civil Liberties Union, while handling numerous cases to improve conditions in prisons for common convicted criminals who have murdered, raped, and plundered, had never handled any aspect of even one case involving a civilly committed patient who had committed no crime, until 1970 when it filed an *amicus curiae* brief in the *Donaldson case.*"[19]

the police, the professions, and American society as a whole accord these individuals the same rights as are accorded anyone else under the equal protections clause of the Fourteenth Amendment. This the Supreme Court has never done for mental patients and has failed to do for Donaldson.

Having lost the case in the courts, the MHLP has tried to re-win it in the press. For instance, Friedman inaccurately proclaimed that state mental hospitals will now have to "re-evaluate all of their involuntarily hospitalized patients to identify non-dangerous individuals who are being held against their will in custodial confinement."[22]

In a later interview with *American Medical News,* Friedman went even further and claimed that the Supreme Court decision in the *Donaldson* case should not be interpreted as a rejection of the concept of the right to treatment:

> [S]ome reports intimate that the decision is a signal to lower courts not to enforce the right to treatment. . . . While it did not specifically endorse the right to treatment, the unanimous opinion did not express any disapproval of the right to treatment.[23]

This attempt to redefine defeat as victory—premised on completely ignoring Chief Justice Burger's separate opinion—seems to me preposterous.

III

A similar misreading and misreporting characterized the handling of the *Donaldson* case in the medical and psychiatric press. For example, on October 1, 1975, *Fron-*

95

tiers of Psychiatry printed a beaming photograph of Donaldson on its front page, with the caption: "Hailing it as 'a victory for common sense,' former mental patient Kenneth Donaldson holds up a copy of the Supreme Court opinion upholding lower court award to him of damages totaling $38,500."[24]

This is a remarkable piece of reporting, as it states exactly the opposite of what in fact happened. Had the Supreme Court denied O'Connor's petition protesting the damages he was ordered to pay, as it had previously denied Donaldson's repeated petitions protesting the hospitalization he was ordered to undergo, then Donaldson would have received $38,500 and the opinion of the Court of Appeals about the constitutionality of a right to treatment for involuntary mental patients would have stood as judicial precedent. The Supreme Court took all this away from Donaldson and his legal champions, and gave them instead a few high-sounding but empty phrases about the post-commitment rights of hypothetical patients.

The story in the July 1975 issue of *Clinical Psychiatry News* was more accurate. After summarizing the facts and the Supreme Court's decision, the anonymous writer went on to note that, "the right to treatment issue was avoided so zealously by the Court that the opinion by Justice Potter Stewart even contained a paragraph saying it was not deciding that issue. There were reports that this was partially to obtain the votes for a unanimous ruling."[25]

Among the experts quoted in this article was Alan Stone, chairman of the American Psychiatric Association's Judiciary Commission, who was said to be "delighted at the portion of the decision that vacated damages against

Dr. O'Connor. This is a real victory for us. The Commission is thrilled."[26]

Judd Marmor, the 1975 president of the APA, acclaimed the ruling as a measure that would put "greater pressure on legislatures to provide more funds that will be necessary to improve the situation," and hence put more of the taxpayers' money into the psychiatrists' pockets.[27]

Bertram Brown, director of the National Institute of Mental Health, took a psycho-political tack of a different sort. Instead of demanding more money for coercive psychiatry, he denied that it constituted a significant problem because, "The number of patients confined involuntarily to whom the decision applies is becoming smaller and smaller in response to the continuing trend toward voluntary admission."[28]

However, in the context of contemporary commitment policies, the actual situation of a so-called voluntary mental hospital patient is more like than unlike that of an involuntary mental hospital patient. In the words of the Utah Supreme Court, "a voluntary patient at the [mental] hospital is as much 'confined' and has as little freedom as a mentally alert trustee in a jail or prison."[29] In short, there really is no such thing as voluntary mental hospitalization, nor can there be so long as there is involuntary mental hospitalization.[30] Brown conveniently ignores this.

Clinical Psychiatry News also contacted O'Connor, who "called the decision 'nothing new' and said that the care offered to Mr. Donaldson was 'so far as we knew adequate at the time.' "[31]

O'Connor was right. The *Donaldson* decision is nothing new and neither are the reactions of psychiatrists to it who have always maintained that they never committed anyone who did not need it.*

In August 1975 *Clinical Psychiatry News* published a follow-up on the *Donaldson* case, which revealed that in the opinion of most hospital psychiatrists, the Supreme Court rendered no decision at all: "Most medical directors and superintendents of mental hospitals in various states of the nation are convinced that the recent decision of the Supreme Court in the Donaldson case will have no effect or only a very slight effect on the operations of their institutions in the future."[33] Typical assessments of the case's impact ranged from "minimal" to "none whatsoever."[34]

One of the better reports on the Donaldson case appeared in *Medical Tribune*. It began by noting that "there were almost as many different opinions expressed on what the high court said and what the consequences will be, as there were experts interviewed."[35]

The report included an interview with Morton Birnbaum, who expressed disappointment at the court's sidestepping of the right to treatment issue, but was pleased over the court's recognition "for the first time [of] mental patients'

---

* In 1961, at a hearing before the Senate Subcommittee on the Constitutional Rights of the Mentally Ill, Winfred Overholser, the then superintendent of St. Elizabeth's Hospital, declared:

> In a discussion of the rights of the mentally ill, unfounded fears have been created regarding possible unlawful deprivation of liberty of the patient. Actually, the public mental hospitals, as instrumentalities of the State, may reasonably be expected to send patients back to the community as soon as their condition warrants, and always *habeas corpus* is available. After 45 years in mental hospitals and their administration, I am convinced that the basis for the belief that persons are improperly sent to mental hospitals is, for pracical purposes, entirely without foundation.[32]

98

rights to *habeas corpus.*"[36] However, the rights of mental patients to habeas corpus was not even an issue in the case. The fact that one of Donaldson's supposed defenders and one of the chief architects of the right-to-treatment doctrine draws this conclusion from the decision tells us something about the mentality of these false friends of the victims of psychiatric slavery: Namely, that instead of trying to abolish slavery, they want to "improve" it. This is borne out by Birnbaum's comment on the *Donaldson* case in *Psychiatric News:*

> Morton Birnbaum, M.D., the father of the right-to-treatment concept, said he is disappointed in the Supreme Court's decision. He anticipated that the Court would attack the right-to-treatment issue; instead it attacked hospitalization, an issue he feels is "relatively unimportant at this time."[37]

Birnbaum is not only consistently wrong-headed but also consistently wrong. The court did not attack hospitalization, and the issue of involuntary mental hospitalization is not unimportant at this time. Birnbaum cuts the pitiful figure of a person pretending to protect the human rights of a victimized group, and yet his every word and deed belie that claim.

IV

As time passed and as journalists studied the *Donaldson* decision more closely, their reports on its implications became more discerning and critical. For example, on August 17, 1975 in a front-page article in *The New York Times*, Boyce Rensberger offered a thoughtful analysis of the practical consequences of the *Donaldson* decision, concluding that the ruling "produced little more than controversies about its narrow and sometimes vague language. . . ."[38] He summarized the decision as mandating that, "a mentally ill person could not be held against his will if the following criteria were met: The hospital was not offering treatment. The person was not dangerous to himself or others. The person was capable of living in the community with the help of friends or relatives."[39]

This summary highlights the hollowness of the opinion. The justices of the Supreme Court devised a ruling that presents as facts or phenomena what, in the real world, are invariably the claims or counterclaims of psychiatrists and patients. There are countless patients who contend that these criteria apply to them and to many other committed patients. But I dare say that there is not a single institutional psychiatrist who would ever admit that any of his patients meet these criteria. In short, the Supreme Court has devised a category of patients who ought to be released from mental hospitals, but the only persons who clearly meet the criteria they have specified are invisible men and women.

After reviewing and remarking on the ambiguities of the key words and concepts identifying each of the three categories listed above—such as therapy, dangerousness, and the capacity to live outside the mental hospital— Rensberger reported the actual, predictable responses of mental health administrators to the ruling: "At present many states have, at least as an initial reaction, said that the decision does not apply to them for one reason or another. One of the more common reasons is that all of their involuntary mental patients are considered dangerous."[40] Rensberger quotes one anonymous psychiatrist observing, cynically but realistically: "You know what that means. . . . You're dangerous if they say you are, and if they want to put you away they say you're dangerous."[41]

There is, certainly, nothing new about this. All this makes it all the móre dismaying that the supposed advocates of the rights of mental patients still are so eager to fight their psychiatrist-adversaries on the latter's grounds and by their rules. It seems that once again the friends of the mental patient have dug an even deeper hole for him.

V

One of the most immediate and interesting legal responses to the *Donaldson* decision was an article by Reginald Stanton in the *New Jersey Law Journal.* Stanton, a judge of the Morris County (N.J.) Court, evidently has had much experience with commitments and has studied the Donaldson decision closely. It is significant, therefore, that he interprets this decision as upholding, above all else, the constitutionality of committing individuals to mental hospitals who are too inept, as judged by psychiatrists and judges, to survive on the outside. According to Judge Stanton:

This is a very important point because I have become increasingly convinced as I deal with patients committed to our mental institutions that most of them are not dangerous in the restricted sense of being a suicide risk or a threat to others. However, they are dangerous to themselves in the broad sense that, if left to themselves, they would not be able to cope and would not survive safely in freedom.[42]

He develops his argument as follows:

I believe that the opinion in *O'Connor* v. *Donaldson* lends some support for my view on the state's right to confine the fundamentally inept mental patient. . . . Note that the Court was not satisfied to treat the patient as being "nondangerous." It carefully spoke of him as a nondangerous person who is "capable of surviving safely in freedom by himself or with the help of willing and responsible family members or friends." I think the fair implication of the language is that a patient need not be released merely because he is "nondangerous" in the sense [that] he is not a suicide risk or a threat to others.[43]

The more closely Stanton analyzes the *Donaldson* decision, and the more vigorously he pushes his justifications for commitment, the more inexorably does he arrive at the conclusion that, instead of constricting the criteria for commitment, the *Donaldson* decision actually expands them! Noting the difficulties that psychiatrists and judges often have in making accurate diagnoses of patients whose commitment is sought, or of predicting their future behavior or dangerousness, Stanton sees the *Donaldson* ruling as offering relief from these uncertainties, resolving doubts about the patient in favor of his commitment and retention. Indeed, he sees the decision as relaxing the justifications for commitment:

I do not believe that it is necessary to settle upon a specific diagnostic label for a patient in order to be satisfied that he is mentally ill. . . . [I]f one treats the concept of dangerousness to self as being broad enough to include the fundamentally inept mental patients, then a very much larger group of persons is subject to involuntary commitment.[44]

If Stanton is right, and I think he may be, then his interpretation lends strong support to my contention that the *Donaldson* decision is hardly the victory for the rights of mental patients which Donaldson and his champions claim it is. Instead, it is still another exercise in psychiatric renaming—that is, calling things that are harmful to patients helpful to them. To the list that has so far included such things as calling prisons "hospitals," wardens "doctors," and prisoners "patients," we may now add calling judicial decisions expanding the criteria for incarcerating persons as madmen a "victory for the civil rights of mental patients." *

VI

In its ruling on the *Donaldson* case, the Supreme Court considered, as we saw, only the so-called post-commitment rights of the involuntarily hospitalized mental patient. It did not consider the rights of the individual to resist being transformed into a committed patient, a status in which he could begin to enjoy the post-commitment rights so generously granted him by the court. The irony

---

* Shortly after the *Donaldson* decision was handed down, another legal commentator observed that "*Donaldson* is but the first step in the Supreme Court's recognition of the post-commitment constitutional rights of institutionalized persons who have been involuntarily incarcerated after constitutionally sound civil commitment proceedings,"[45] an interpretation that confirms the impression that the court strengthened, rather than weakened, psychiatric slavery.

of this legal posture is displayed dramatically by the case of a committed patient whose plight made the pages of the daily papers only a few weeks after the *Donaldson* decision was handed down.

In April 1975 Robert Friedman, aged forty-three, was arrested in a Chicago bus station for panhandling. In a briefcase he carried with him the police found $24,087 in small bills. Instead of being charged with a crime or released, Friedman was "ordered committed to a mental institution by a judge who said he was protecting Friedman from possible harm by thugs who might be after the cash he carried." [46] On August 4, 1975 when Friedman's predicament was reported in the press, he was still confined in a psychiatric institution, his predicament unaffected—perhaps even aggravated—by the benefits supposedly bestowed on people like him by the Supreme Court.

Why was Friedman committed? In this case, we need not make conjectures about it. Explained Judge Lawrence L. Genesen at a hearing after Friedman was committed: "I wonder what my decision would have been if he wasn't carrying $24,000 around. On the evidence, I decided that the man lacked good judgment. If he only had a quarter instead of $24,000, my interpretation of his judgment might have been somewhat different." [47]

Judge Genesen was here applying the doctrine of *parens patriae*. Friedman was the helpless child, and he, the judge, the parent who was protecting him. But why by commitment? Did commitment really protect Friedman's life, liberty, and property? Actually, in seeking to protect Friedman's liberty, the judge deprived him of it. In protecting Friedman's property, he confiscated it from him. According to a newspaper report of the case, "Friedman, 43, has seen half his life savings eaten away by hospital fees and doctor's bills for treatment ordered by the court and by an $800-a-month drain the state says it costs to keep him at the mental facility he fought to stay out of. He was even ordered to pay the fees for a lawyer who argued that he be committed." [48]

There is, again, nothing new about any of this. It is why the doctrine of *parens patriae* could never be applied properly to the psychiatric area, and why it cannot now be applied properly to it. Friedman, it should be noted, is getting just the treatment that David Bazelon, Morton Birnbaum, the ACLU, the APA, the MHLP, and all the other enlightened supporters of the right-to-treatment doctrine have demanded: He is getting treated at a cost of $800 per month, whether he likes it or not. When Friedman sues, he will not be able to say, as Donaldson did, that he got no treatment. He got the best treatment the great city of Chicago has to offer its madmen.

I warned some time ago that the only thing worse than commitment is commitment safeguarded by the right to treatment.[49] The parody of psychiatric care that has surfaced in the case of Lawrence Friedman supports this rather obvious concern and easy prediction. However, the Friedman case is important not only as heart-rending evidence contradicting the claims of the right-to-treatment advocates, but also as a mirror in which we might see, ever so clearly, the boundless hypocrisy of psychiatric paternalism and the horrible brutality of psychiatric justice. Consider the following paradoxes.

Friedman is committed on the grounds that he is a danger to himself. How is he a danger to himself? By carrying a large sum of money on his person, which is his right. But this endangers him because the "normal" people of Chicago might steal his money, and in the process of robbing him these "normal" people might injure or kill him.

Assuming that Judge Genesen wanted to protect Friedman from these hazards, he actually had several options: First, he might have warned Friedman of the unwisdom of his conduct, and let him go; second, he might have suggested that Friedman deposit most of his money in a bank and pocket only so much of it as he needed from day to day or week to week; third, he might have ordered Friedman to bank his money or face commitment; and finally, he might have provided Friedman with police guards to protect him from the illegal acts of the "normal" citizens of Chicago. No doubt one could think of other possible responses, individual and societal, to the problem Friedman posed for Judge Genesen and the city of Chicago. None, however, would be as pleasing and profitable to the practitioners of psychiatric justice as is civil commitment—especially when the committed mental patient is guaranteed the benefits of his constitutional right to treatment.

VII

This review of popular, psychiatric, and legal reactions to the Supreme Court's ruling in the *Donaldson* case amply supports my contention that the case was widely misread and misreported. Although this phenomenon is itself a subject worth exploring further, I will limit myself here to the conjecture that it is a result of the Supreme Court's own ambivalence toward the case. The court's opinion supported neither petitioner nor respondent and was, in fact, a non-decision.

In view of the actual relations between institutional

psychiatrists and institutionalized mental patients—which resembles closely the relations between unhappily married couples—the court's hesitancy about assigning blame to either party is understandable. In the bad marriage between psychiatrist and psychotic, to which the public is inevitably witness, each party has its legitimate grievances. Psychiatrists revile psychotics, psychotics revile psychiatrists, and the public—composed partly of psychiatrists and psychotics and partly of others whose behavior is not much better—would like to rid itself of the nuisance these querulants create as easily and cheaply as possible (which usually means maintaining the status quo). It is tempting, indeed, to conclude that each party has brought its misery on itself.[50] Historically and psychologically there is much merit in that conclusion, but morally we must reject it. Why? Because that is the essence of becoming civilized: eschewing interpersonal coercion through force and fraud and replacing it with cooperation through contract and self-control.

In everyday life we do not let people use the state's police power for settling any or all disagreements. People annoy and insult each other all the time, but as a rule they must live with each other as best they can, or separate. In the last analysis, psychiatric incarceration, although it is usually in a public hospital through a publicly administered procedure, is nevertheless a sort of private imprisonment sanctioned by the state. It is a relic of confinement in the private madhouse, an arrangement at which the law had long gazed with unseeing eyes. When at last, in the nineteenth century, the law began to look, it refused to believe the evidence of its senses, proclaiming that the fault with private psychiatric confinement was not that it was confinement but that it was private.[50]

The upshot was the erection of elaborate legal safeguards against the abuse of involuntary mental hospitalization, bestowing a far-reaching legal and medical legitimization on the practice of depriving innocent people of their liberty. This explains why combating this practice without opposing the legitimizations that support it has been so fruitless, and why it is bound to remain so.

8

A Right to Treatment
or a Right to Treat?

I

The subject of the mental patient's so-called right to treatment has received much attention in recent years. It is impossible to assign an exact date to the origin of this idea, as the notion is clearly coeval with the practice of mad-doctoring.[1] Ever since the seventeenth century, when psychiatry in its modern sense began, madness was conceived of as some sort of malady, and the madman was viewed as someone who does not know his own best interests. It was an integral part of this image that the madman ought to be cared for by others. Although this care consisted of brutal confinement, this seemingly altruistic idea became increasingly attractive to its purveyors and to the public. From the start, then, the madman's right to care was, in fact, the mad-doctor's right to confine him; and now the plea for the mental patient's right to treatment is, in effect, a plea for the psychiatrist's right to treat him.

Although it is difficult to discuss the right to treatment without considering what constitutes treatment and what the disease is for which it is supposed to be a remedy, I shall resist the temptation to take up this subject here. Suffice it to say that a great deal of so-called psychiatric treatment has as its aim a change in the patient's beliefs and behavior. Regardless of their particular psychiatric persuasion, most psychiatrists—and most non-psychiatrists —agree with this view. If such change of belief occurs voluntarily—with the subject's consent and, indeed, with his active cooperation—then it presents no special moral, legal, or constitutional issue. This sort of personality change falls readily into the general category of learning.[2] However, what if such change in belief is imposed on a person against his will? It then presents a very obvious moral, legal, and constitutional problem.* If coerced per-

---

* More than a half-century ago, Karl Jaspers, the great German psychiatrist-turned-philosopher, emphasized that the concept of treatment is not applicable to so-called psychotics:

> Rational treatment is not really an attainable goal as regards the large majority of mental patients in the strict sense. . . . Admission to hospital often takes place against the will of the patient and therefore the psychiatrist finds himself in a different relation to his patient than other doctors. He tries to make this difference as negligible as possible by deliberately emphasizing his purely medical approach to the patient, but the latter in many cases is quite convinced that he is well and resists these medical efforts.[3]

Nevertheless, contemporary psychiatrists and jurists prattle not

sonality change affects religious belief or conduct, then it clearly conflicts with the First Amendment guarantee of freedom of religion. How, then, should coerced psychiatric personality change be viewed?

I do not see how it is possible to deny that coerced psychiatric personality change—even (or especially) if it entails "helping" a person to give up his "psychotic delusions"—closely resembles coerced religious conversion. If so, it is obvious not only that there can be no such thing as a "right" to involuntary psychiatric treatment, such as Bazelon, Birnbaum, Ennis, and others are advocating, but that such an involuntary intervention is itself a clear constitutional "wrong."[4] The Supreme Court actually gave a ringing affirmation of this view in a suit concerning whether the state can require Jehovah's Witnesses to salute the flag. The court reasoned that such a salute "require(s) the affirmation of a belief and an attitude of mind" which it is constitutionally impermissible to create by coercion.[5] In phrases that I submit are applicable equally to coerced psychiatric treatment, the court declared that,

> (I)f there is any fixed star in our constitutional constellation, it is that no official, high or petty, can prescribe what shall be orthodox in politics, nationalism, religion, or other matters of opinion, or force citizens to confess by word or action their faith therein. If there are any circumstances which permit an exception, they do not now occur to us.[6]

----

merely about the treatment of just such individuals but also about their right to it.

As befits an *inimicus curiae,* I would like to remind the justices of the Supreme Court of what evidently never occurred to them: namely, that they have always made an exception to this rule in the case of psychiatry. In fact, what never even occurred to the justices is that involuntary psychiatric treatment constitutes an instance of "forcing citizens to confess by word or act their faith" in a social reality interpreted by institutional psychiatry. Therein, precisely, lies the tragedy of psychiatric slavery.

II

Although the idea of depriving persons of liberty on the grounds of insanity is not of American origin, it fell on fertile soil in the United States. We are thus confronted with an astonishing, seemingly paradoxical, spectacle: Namely, that although American political reformers have done more to enlarge and secure individual liberty than has any such group anywhere in the world, American psychiatric reformers have done more to constrict and endanger it than has any such group anywhere in the world. From Benjamin Rush and Isaac Ray, through Dorothea Dix and the crooks of the "cult of curability," to Alexander, Menninger, Bazelon, and the other terrorists of the Therapeutic State—American psychiatric reform has been characterized by an implacable hostility to individual dignity, liberty, and responsibility, and by a corresponding zeal to replace personal self-control with the controls of pseudo-medical despots.[7] A few citations from the writings of some psychiatric "greats" will illustrate how well they loved, not liberty, but psychiatry.

In 1783 Benjamin Rush, the undisputed father of American psychiatry, whose portrait adorns the official seal of the American Psychiatric Association, wrote to a friend: "Mankind considered as creatures made for immortality are worthy of all our cares. Let us view them as patients in a hospital. The more they resist our efforts, the more they have need of our services." [8]

Rush's life and writings reveal him to be a zealous therapeutic inquisitor who would have made many a theological inquisitor seem tame by comparison. He declared his own son insane and locked him up in his own hospital, where the son languished, except for one brief "remission," for twenty-seven years.[9] On January 2, 1811 Rush wrote to Jefferson: "He [John] is now in a cell in the Pennsylvania Hospital, where there is too much reason to believe he will end his days." [10]

As for Rush's criteria for commitment, he articulated them in his classical *Medical Inquiries and Observations upon the Diseases of the Mind,* hailed by psychiatrists as the first American textbook of psychiatry, as follows:

Miss H. L. . . . was confined in our hospital in the year 1800. For several weeks she [displayed] every mark of a sound mind, except one. She hated her father. On a certain day, she acknowledged, with pleasure, a return of her filial attachment and affection for him; soon after she was discharged cured.[11]

The next "giant" in American psychiatry, Isaac Ray, offered this opinion in 1838 about the constitutional limits that ought to be placed on the deprivation of personal freedom under psychiatric auspices:

When the restoration of the patient is the object sought for, as it always is or should be, in recent cases, no unnecessary restrictions should be imposed on this measure. The simple fact of the recency of the case should be sufficient, when properly attested, to warrant his seclusion, if it be deemed necessary for his care.[12]

These phrases recur with remarkably little change throughout the rest of psychiatric history and are advanced today as if they constituted a novel and revolutionary scientific program. At the core of Ray's recommendation for involuntary mental hospitalization lay a clear reordering of moral and political priorities—the promise of mental restoration in the asylum displacing the problems of personal liberty in society. As classic liberals and modern libertarians want a minimum of "unnecessary restrictions" on individual freedom, so institutional psychiatrists and psychiatrically enlightened jurists want a minimum of such restrictions on therapeutic coercions.

In 1929 Franz Alexander actually committed this horror to paper:

The neurotic criminal obviously has a limited sense of responsibility. Primarily he is a sick person. . . . If he is curable, he should be incarcerated for the duration of psychiatric treatment so long as he still represents a menace to society. If he is incurable, he belongs in a hospital for incurables for life.[3]

For three decades following the publication of the foregoing sentences, Alexander was one of the most respected and influential psychiatrists and psychoanalysts in the United States.

Karl Menninger, himself one of Alexander's students—who went on to become the acknowledged dean of American psychiatry in the 1950s and 1960s—has continued to spread the gospel of social security through institutional psychiatry. Menninger is an enthusiastic advocate of preventive psychiatric detention. He advocates replacing penal sanctions with psychiatric sanctions—claiming even that although punishment is a crime, crime is a disease:

Eliminating one offender who happens to get caught *weakens* public scrutiny by creating a false sense of diminished danger through a definite remedial measure. Actually, it does not remedy anything, and it bypasses completely the real and unsolved problem of *how to identify, detect, and detain potentially dangerous citizens* (emphasis in the original).[14]

Karl Menninger, president of the American Psychiatric Association, uncompromising advocate of psychiatric coercion, and the proprietor-leader of a famous private insane asylum named after his family, has occupied and continues to occupy a prominent position in the American Civil Liberties Union.

III

David Bazelon is one of the most prominent advocates of psychiatric coercion concealed as care and cure. He has succeeded in deforming liberty by ostensibly reforming criminology and psychiatry—an enterprise whose worth he has gravely misjudged, partly by thinking that it is good when it is evil, and partly by believing that it rests on new discoveries when in fact it rests on old deceptions.* Thus in 1960 Bazelon offered this plea for psychiatric-legal reform:

> When the sentence has been served, the warden of the penitentiary signs a certificate to that effect, and the prisoner rejoins society—even though it may be obvious that the punishment has worked no cure. . . . On the other hand, the inmate of a mental hospital is released only when certified by the staff as cured, or at least not dangerous to himself or others. . . . Is it not evident that treatment rather than punitive incarceration offers society better protection? [16]

O'Connor and Gumanis acted on just these principles in treating Donaldson, and many of Bazelon's fellow jurists reared up in righteous indignation against them.

By 1967 Judge Bazelon had managed to get rid of personal choice and will altogether. In this process he also disposed of the individual, as we know this concept and use this term when we speak of individual freedom and responsibility:

> Scientists now generally agree [and Bazelon is obviously agreeing with them] that human behavior is caused rather than willed. . . . What is usually required of the [psychiatric] expert is a statement in simple terms of why the accused acted as he did— the psychodynamics of his behavior. . . . Where it occurs, under the Durham rule [handed down by

---

* In *Make Mad the Guilty,* Richard Arens documented how, in his quest for psychiatric salvation, Judge David Bazelon's judicial decisions have sacrificed both common sense and civil liberties.[15]

Bazelon], the accused may be seen as a sick person and confined to a hospital for treatment, not to prison for punishment.[17]

Here it is in its naked horror: one of the most widely known and respected American judges advocating that persons accused of offenses be deprived of their constitutional right to trial by defining them as mad and locking them up in the madhouse. Indeed, as a judge, Bazelon has not only advocated this course of action but has also practiced it. It is not surprising that he is a much-decorated hero in the struggle for psychiatric justice, having received both a Certificate of Commendation and the Isaac Ray Award from the American Psychiatric Association. In 1970 Bazelon served as the President of the American Orthopsychiatric Association, one of the constituent bodies of the Mental Health Law Project—the "psychiatric liberties" group that shepherded the *Donaldson* case through the courts. In 1967 Bazelon was a leading member of an official United States Mission on Mental Health to Russia. In the Soviet Union, Bazelon saw nothing of the much-heralded Communist abuse of psychiatry but saw much to admire and praise. The following passage from his report on that trip conveys both his judgment of Soviet psychiatry and his position on involuntary mental hospitalization:

[I]nstitutionalization is a significant part of the Russian approach. Even if a patient opposes hospital commitment, it is deemed voluntary if it is sought by the patient's family, his trade union, business organization, or polyclinic doctor. The Russian attitude seems to be that under these circumstances the patient himself would want hospitalization if he could make rational decisions. As a result, only three or four percent of all commitments are termed involuntary. I must hasten to add that many of our own psychiatrists share the same underlying attitude. . . . They justify this on the ground that they are acting for the patient's benefit. . . . And, of course, these psychiatrists may be right. Perhaps people who need treatment should be involuntarily hospitalized for their own benefit, even if they are not dangerous. But clearly this is a decision which must be made by society as a whole—not by the psychiatric profession alone or by individual psychiatrists.[18]

Nothing could show more clearly how devout a believer Bazelon is in mental illness and the psychiatric cures for it. He accepts as a given, as something too obvious to challenge, that every civilized society must have involuntary mental hospitalization. Indeed it is so important that just as war must not be left to the generals alone, so commitment must not be left to the psychiatrist alone: The decision must be made by society as a whole.

To be sure, Bazelon's views on psychiatric incarceration are not original: They are simply the faithful reflections, undistorted by doubt, of the prevailing psychiatric imbecility in the mirror of judicial inhumanity. To illustrate the extent to which psychiatric incarceration forms the backbone of official psychiatry, I want to cite a typical passage from *Noyes' Modern Clinical Psychiatry* (Seventh Edition), whose author, Lawrence C. Kolb, was for many years professor of psychiatry at Columbia University and is now the Commissioner of Mental Hygiene in New York State. In a chapter on "Personality Disorders," under the section "Sexual Deviation," Kolb offers these revealing remarks:

> If the offender has not been guilty of violence, it is usually desirable that he be confined in a hospital atmosphere. . . . Through therapy and subsequent parole, some such offenders, if their desire for improvement is strong, may be enabled to channel their impulses into constructive activities.[19]

Exactly what sort of non-violent sex criminals is Kolb referring to here? In the three pages immediately preceding the passage quoted, he presents the pathology and treatment of the following sexual deviations: homosexuality, pedophilia, fetishism, transvestism, and exhibitionism. It is the non-violent practitioners of any or all of these perversions, then, that Kolb believes are best treated by coerced psychiatry and parole. His opinion, as befits so sage an expert, is of course not his alone. In support of it, he cites the recommendations of the most liberal and enlightened division of all the branches of the psychiatric establishment, a clique that has aptly called itself the Group for the Advancement of Psychiatry (GAP). Here is what Kolb cites from a 1949 GAP pamphlet, *Psychiatrically Deviated Sex Offenders:* "If the offender is curable he can be eventually released to society; if not, he should never be released. . . . The Committee is unreserved in its opinion that the committed sex offender should be actively treated in a non-penal institution."[20]

If this sounds like Franz Alexander's classic totalitarian line about neurotic criminals, it is because the members of GAP who wrote it probably derived their ideas from Alexander. It is important to note that the GAP is unreserved in its endorsement of coerced psychiatric treatment; that Kolb is unreserved in his endorsement of this position; and that Kolb's book is the most authoritative and widely used text in American medical schools and psychiatric residency programs. Such, then, is the "official" American psychiatric position on psychiatric justice and psychiatric slavery.

IV

At the present time the chief interpreter of and spokesman for the official American psychiatric position on matters concerning law and psychiatry is Alan Stone, Professor of Law and Psychiatry at Harvard University, and the chairman of the American Psychiatric Association's Commission on Judicial Action. When Christianity was an established faith in the West, leading theologians distinguished themselves by writing Christian apologetics. Today, when psychiatry is an established faith, leading psychiatrists distinguish themselves by writing psychiatric apologetics.

After the Supreme Court handed down its ruling on the *Donaldson* case, Stone wrote a review of the history and present status of the concept of the right to treatment, unequivocally supporting it.[21] Why does he like it? Because it supports the medical legitimacy of psychiatry, is a useful vehicle for seeking more public funding for psychiatry, and offers a justification for urging the liquidation of the private practice of medicine and its replacement by national health insurance.

Stone cogently observes that in the history of the early right-to-treatment cases, "not one of them arose in the context of the more numerous and familiar cases of civil commitment of the mentally ill. All of the cases involved men who, although diverted from the prison system into hospitals, had been originally charged with crimes."[22]

From this Stone infers that because they were charged with crimes, all these men "had extensive access to legal counsel"; which, in turn, "is illustrative of the lawyer's contention that without the right to counsel all other rights are bootless."[23]

I submit a different inference, namely that these cases illustrate the propensity in forensic psychiatry to remedy one injustice by adding another one to it. The problem in these cases lay not in the lack of treatment but in the diversion from the criminal process. If lawyers, psychiatrists, and civil libertarians had insisted that persons charged with crimes ought to be tried, sentenced if guilty, and discharged by the courts if innocent, the very problem of people languishing in mental hospitals as quasi-criminals would never have arisen.

When these problems did arise, they inexorably brought with them their own solution: the newly discovered constitutional right to treatment. Thus, according to Stone, in the celebrated case of *Rouse* v. *Cameron*, "Judge Bazelon found the right to treatment in his interpretation of the statute of the District of Columbia, [and] indicated there might be a constitutional right as well; he alluded to the question of cruel and unusual punishment and of due process and equal protection of the laws."[24]

Judge Bazelon did not, however, allude to the possibility that diversion from the criminal to the psychiatric route of social control was itself unconstitutional! In other words, he preferred to fashion a *new* constitutional right for these persons incarcerated in insane asylums rather than to find the established constitutional right to trial applicable to their cases.[25]

I want to recall at this point the Fifth Circuit's decision in *Donaldson,* as it was premised on the concept of the right to treatment; and to note some of the problems, so far not considered, which such a quasi-medical approach to involuntary mental patients raises. The central claim that *Donaldson* placed before the Court of Appeals—and which that court upheld, but the Supreme Court rejected —was that "Where nondangerous patient is involuntarily committed under civil commitment procedures to state mental hospital, only constitutionally permissible purpose of confinement is to provide treatment and patient has due process right to such treatment as will help him to be cured or to improve his mental condition."[26]

This claim is a tissue of nonsense, and a dense one at that. I say this because it seeks to justify depriving an innocent person of liberty on the grounds that he is mentally ill and will receive treatment for it, a reasoning that implies—as essentially unchallengeable—that the subject has, in fact, an illness; that it is treatable; that the treatment will be forthcoming; and that it will be effective. Actually, each of these premises may be false. The "patient" may not have an illness at all, for example, because "mental illness" is not an illness; or he may not have the illness imputed to him, although such an illness exists, because he was falsely diagnosed; or, once confined, he may not be treated; or the treatment may be ineffective or even harmful.

What procedural protection is there, in a ruling such as was advanced in behalf of Donaldson, to protect healthy persons against false diagnoses of illness? Doctors are fallible human beings. Mistaken diagnoses are an ever-present medical possibility. Who shall bear the risk of such error in cases where the very act of making a diagnosis is imposed involuntarily on the so-called patient?

The risks of diagnosing and treating disease are generally well appreciated. They are borne by patients, or would-be patients, in the hope that future medical benefits will accrue to them. Where such hope is absent—for example, in the fatally ill person—permission for further diagnostic explorations is often withheld, and wisely so. Once the diagnostic intervention is wrenched out of its traditional voluntary context, the very word "diagnosis" loses its meaning. For if the consequence of a positive finding of mental illness is psychiatric confinement, and if such confinement is undesired, the persons subjected to diagnostic studies of mental illness would inevitably regard the intervention not as diagnosis but as self-incrimination. If a person accused of a crime for which the penalty is only a fine has, nevertheless, a right against self-incrimination, how could that right be denied a person accused of a mental illness for which the treatment is incarceration? If, however, the right against self-incrimination is extended from the penal context to the psychiatric, then in all cases of involuntary psychiatric interventions, there will be a fresh conflict between two constitutional rights—the right against self-incrimination and the right to treatment. Which of these rights ought then to prevail? The right-to-treatment advocates stubbornly evade such questions. Instead, they extoll the obvious nobility of their cause, as does Stone when he writes:

The constitutional right to treatment has now become an accepted part of our legal order, but it lacks the imprimatur of the Supreme Court. . . . The Supreme Court actually dealt with the [*Donaldson*] case in a manner that leaves all the important right to treatment questions unanswered.[27]

Thus, neither the fact that *Donaldson* left all the important right to treatment questions unanswered, nor Chief Justice Burger's opposition to the concept of the right to treatment dampens Stone's enthusiasm for the idea. "There is," he remarks approvingly, "already an avalanche of decisions [affirming a right to treatment] in every area of noncriminal confinement."[28] The practical implications of the doctrine, as Stone sees them, are painfully familiar —that is, a demand and a justification for more tax monies for institutional psychiatry:

> In the end the real solution to the problems addressed by the right to treatment cannot come from complicated judicial discourse about civil rights and civil liberties. It must come in the form of a system of national health insurance that includes adequate mental health coverage for inpatient as well as outpatient treatment and for chronic as well as acute mental illness. To some, this will seem unrealistic or too expensive or too much like socialized medicine. But is there a humane alternative that psychiatrists can endorse?[29]

Yes. Leaving people alone. Offering them help but eschewing coercion.

V

It seems fitting to conclude this critique of the concept of the right to treatment with a careful consideration of the views of Morton Birnbaum, the man often said to be the proud father of this anencephalic monster.* Birnbaum began his campaign for the right to treatment in 1960, from an observation that is both valid and important—namely, that people in public mental hospitals generally do not receive what one ordinarily would regard as medical treatment. There are at least two immediate and obvious conclusions that might be drawn from this observation. One is that such hospitals are medical institutions in name only. The other is that they are *bona fide* medical institutions in which more medical treatment ought to be dispensed. I drew, and continue to draw, the first conclusion. Birnbaum drew, and continues to draw, the second.

In 1960 in an article in the *American Bar Association Journal* Birnbaum advocated "the recognition and enforcement of the legal right of a mentally ill inmate of a public mental institution to adequate medical treatment of his mental illness."[31]

In 1963 in *Law, Liberty, and Psychiatry* I rejected this proposal because, "it supported the myth that mental illness is a medical problem that can be solved by medical

---

* In view of the historical record of psychiatry, current claims for a right to treatment for the institutionalized mentally ill, especially as advanced by Bazelon and Birnbaum and their followers, are simply absurd and obscene. These psychiatric reformers write and talk as if their proposal for a right to treatment were a new scientific and humanitarian idea. Actually, more than one hundred years ago, the national association of American madhouse keepers agitated for what were, in effect, right-to-treatment laws. In 1868, in a unanimous resolution, the members of the Association of Medical Superintendents of American Institutions for the Insane, declared that "believing that certain relations of the insane should be regulated by statutory enactments calculated to secure their rights . . . [we] recommend that the following legal provisions be adopted by every state whose existing laws do not, already, satisfactorily provide for these great ends."[30]

125

means."[32] Furthermore, I view the care provided by compulsory mental treatment as potentially much more harmful than the metaphorical disease it is supposed to cure.

Despite the millions of words that have since been said and written for and against the right to treatment, the argument has advanced very little. I continue to insist that, because it is an evil like slavery, involuntary psychiatry should be abolished. Birnbaum continues to insist that, because it is a good like curing the disease of an unconscious patient, the involuntary treatment of the involuntary mental patient should be a right guaranteed and enforced by the courts.

As fresh evidence that mental illness is unlike bodily illness keeps cropping up, Birnbaum and I continue to interpret it in diametrically opposite ways. Obsessed with the idea of the right to treatment, Birnbaum declares—as if saying it made it so—that "Medicaid and Medicare statutes are in reality federal right-to-treatment statutes."[33] In fact, Medicaid and Medicare are methods of third-party payment for various medical interventions many of which may not be therapeutic, such as diagnostic procedures or hospitalization of the dying patient. But never mind; to Birnbaum everything that doctors do is treatment.

Having offered his personal definition of Medicare and Medicaid, Birnbaum indignantly declares: "I was quite surprised that in 1965 the initial Medicaid legislation . . . totally excluded only one group among the nation's poor and infirm: state mental hospital patients under 65."[34] That is a fact. Again, the question is: What shall we make of it? What Birnbaum makes of it is that "This is simply another example of how a sanist Congress elected by a sanist society handles this most complex problem in planning to deliver adequate health care to our nation."[35] What I make of it is that this is another example supporting the view that the status of state mental hospital inmates is more like that of children than of adult medical patients. Since such state mental hospital patients are, ostensibly, already cared for by the state, as *parens patriae,* Congress has concluded that there is no need for additional support for them.

Birnbaum, however, is incensed at this exclusion, perhaps the more so because he keeps telling himself it is all due to what he labels "sanism": "As I believe that the decision was incorrect and was sanist, I am now [1974] considering further petitioning of Congress to end this exclusion, filing a formal complaint with the United Nations Human Rights Council concerning Congressional sanism."[36] This threat is at once ridiculous and repellent. Birnbaum actually proposes to denounce his own country, still the freest in the world, to that bastion of super-morality, the United Nations! Are the Russians and their allies, who after all are quite influential in the U.N., not also "sanist"? Are they so nice to mental patients? Birnbaum's belief that the U.N. is more compassionate or moral than the U.S. Congress is, I submit, deeply revealing of his fundamental hostility to traditional American values of individual freedom and dignity.

On September 25, 1975 *The New York Times* reported on a new case filed by Birnbaum that seems to support the worst charges of psychiatric totalitarianism that could be brought against him. According to this story, Birnbaum has filed suit against federal and New York State officials in a case designated as *Woe* v. *Weinberger* (Woe being the pseudonym of the patient and Weinberger being Caspar Weinberger, the former Secretary of Health, Education, and Welfare), contending that the plaintiff had been committed against his will to the Brooklyn State Hospital where he is receiving care that costs $25 a day. "Dr. Birnbaum argues that the court that committed Mr. Woe could have sent him to the psychiatric ward of Downstate Medical Center across the street, where psychiatric care costs $250 a day. . . But because Downstate . . . will not accept involuntary patients, Mr. Woe went to the state hospital."[37]

Birnbaum's posture is naively self-incriminating. A self-declared champion of the rights of the mentally ill, he is here championing the rights of involuntarily hospitalized mental patients to affirm their identities through their illnesses, and by means of a kind of psychiatric affirmative action program, their right to demand the most expensive treatment available for their diseases.

VI

Urging a right to treatment for involuntarily hospitalized mental patients commits one, linguistically and logically, to accept, first, that there is such a thing as mental illness; second, that persons afflicted with such an illness may be legitimately incarcerated in mental hospitals; and third, that such involuntary patients can be effectively treated by means of psychiatric treatments. Each of these propositions is highly questionable, to say the least. I articulate them here to re-emphasize that Birnbaum embraces all of them with the greatest enthusiasm.

Significantly, Birnbaum's suit is based on the claim that his client was harmed not *by being committed* to the Brooklyn State Hospital, but *by not being committed* to the Downstate Medical Center!

The Downstate Medical Center is the name of the medical school and affiliated hospitals of the State University of New York in Brooklyn. Because of its university affiliation, this hospital is a prestigious institution. The fact that such an institution refuses to accept involuntary mental patients—a practice unheard of a few decades ago —betokens a changing view of commitment among some leading psychiatrists. If one wanted to be optimistic, one might even speculate that today's refusal by some university and private hospitals to admit involuntary mental patients may be a harbinger of tomorrow's general rejection of this practice. Whether such a change is in the air or not, Birnbaum comes down squarely for the preservation, and indeed extension, of the practice of involuntary mental hospitalization.

Birnbaum charges that his client, Mr. Woe, requires involuntary confinement in a mental hospital; and he charges, further, that he should rightly be confined at the Downstate Medical Center. The real object of Birnbaum's argument can therefore be one thing and one thing only: a demand for state intervention to correct such psychiatric discrimination by ordering the Downstate Medical Center (and similar institutions) to admit involuntary mental patients.

This proposition is exquisitely ironic. In all my years in psychiatry, I have never heard even the most ardent institutional psychiatrist complain about hospitals that refuse to admit involuntary patients. Now, Birnbaum, stalwart defender of the mental patient, complains about precisely this breach in the psychiatric front. His demand, in *Woe* v. *Weinberger,* is:

That a declaratory judgment be entered that the involuntarily civilly committed must constitutionally be integrated with the voluntarily hospitalized in the separate, unequal, and superior general hospital psychiatric facilities where they can receive the adequate and active care they need, and which is constitutionally required.[38]

In short, Birnbaum now demands, first, that the courts compel mental hospitals—both public and private—to admit involuntary mental patients; second, that voluntary and involuntary mental patients be compulsorily integrated; and third, by implication, that psychiatrists practicing in mental hospitals (and perhaps even those not so practicing) be compelled to accept involuntary subjects as their patients. These fresh demands in the name of the right to treatment are, indeed, the inexorable consequences of the paternalistic-psychiatric imagery inherent in this doctrine. That they are advanced just at this moment in the history of the struggle between the psychiatric totalitarians and the psychiatric libertarians is of the greatest symbolic significance.

Like many people, Birnbaum believes that some people are so seriously mentally ill that they must be confined in mental hospitals against their will. This belief, as I suggested, is like the belief that some people are so subhuman or childlike that they must be enslaved. The ideology behind slavery requires that, ideally, all blacks be slaves and that all whites who can afford it be slave owners. If some blacks are free and survive in freedom, the ideology is threatened. And if some whites reject slave holding, the ideology is threatened even more. All this was clear enough during the days of Negro slavery in America. Hence, for example, the fugitive slave laws.

To uphold the dignity of the glorious institution of psychiatric slavery, Birnbaum is now suing the United States government, claiming that his client was deprived of his constitutional rights because some psychiatrists refused to accept him as a committed patient. The logic behind this is sound: If every psychiatrist treated involuntary mental patients, whether voluntarily or under state compulsion, then the hands of all psychiatrists would be equally bloody. It would be less likely that any would then object to the practice. At present a few psychiatrists reject psychiatric slavery as immoral, refuse to participate in the psychiatric slave trade, and either try to help psychiatric slaves escape to freedom, or, if the slaves prefer a secure bondage to an uncertain liberty, leave them alone. These psychiatric abolitionists represent an intolerable threat, at once practical and symbolic, to the psychiatric slave holders. Birnbaum endeavors to rid psychiatry of this threat: His aim is not to liberate the involuntary mental patient but to enslave the voluntary psychiatric patient (by compulsorily integrating him with the involuntary mental patient) and the free-market psychiatrist as well (by compulsorily transforming him into a court-dominated slavemaster of his psychiatric slave-patient).

All this is in the best tradition of paternalistic social reformers who cannot tolerate human differences, which they first call inequalities, then inequities, and finally deprivations of constitutional rights. The upshot is that if they cannot raise the black man to the level of the white, or the poor to that of the rich, or the sick to that of the healthy, they can at least reduce the latter to where, in each case, he is indistinguishable from the former. So it is now with the differences between the sane and the insane. Mental health reformers like Birnbaum and the MHLP are not satisfied with setting the insane free by abolishing psychiatric slavery. Why not? Because it would leave many mentally ill individuals palpably still less well off than some other persons not so categorized. What these therapeutic totalitarians want is not freedom but equality. This is why what they advocate is not the abolition of psychiatric coercion but the abolition of the psychiatric inequities between the sane and the insane and between various classes of the insane. By claiming that we ought to protect involuntarily committed mental patients from "deprivations of their constitutional rights to treatment," they are leading us further down the road toward the Therapeutic State.

9

Chattel Slavery and Psychiatric Slavery

I

In its decision in *O'Connor* v. *Donaldson*, the United States Supreme Court held for the respondent on the ground that he was compulsorily confined in a mental hospital even though he was not dangerous.[1] What should we make of this decision? How should we judge the judges and their judgments?

Suppose that in 1855 there had come before the Supreme Court the case of a slave named Donaldson who, having escaped from the South to one of the free states, was suing his former master, O'Connor, for damages for illegal imprisonment. Suppose, further, that the court had decided the case narrowly—that is, without addressing itself to the issue of slavery—saying something like this: Since Donaldson was not chattel, and since as a slave he was deprived of work and kept in idleness, there was no justification for holding him in bondage. Would this have been a good decision? The answer depends on one's point of view.

If one believed that Negroes should be enslaved only because they are chattels and only in order to make them work, then one would have wholeheartedly endorsed the decision. If one believed that Negroes should be enslaved because they are black, and because slavery is a glorious institution indispensable for the integrity of our nation, then one would have opposed the decision. Finally, if one believed that Negroes should not be enslaved at all—indeed that no one should be—because there can be no slavery in a free society, then one would have regarded the decision ambivalently: good, because it diminishes, albeit ever so slightly, the power of the institution of slavery; and bad, because it implicitly legitimizes the practices of this institution, which are incompatible with the moral principles on which our society rests.

The same reasoning and conclusions apply to the *Donaldson* case. Replace involuntary servitude with involuntary psychiatry, blackness with schizophrenia, being chattel with being dangerous, work with treatment— and you have the same situation.

By deciding the case as it did, the court simultaneously weakened psychiatric slavery and strengthened it.

It weakened it by holding, explicitly, that if the patient/ slave is non-dangerous/non-chattel, and is not receiving treatment/is not working, then he may not be confined/

enslaved. It strengthened it by holding, implicitly, that if the patient/slave is dangerous/chattel, and is receiving treatment/is working, then he may be confined/enslaved.

Perhaps some will object to this analogy on the ground that being a chattel and being dangerous are not analogous. But from the point of view of whether a person should or should not be deprived of liberty, they are. Both are strategic ascriptions justifying such deprivations. People do not come into the world labeled "chattel" and "not chattel," "schizophrenic," and "not schizophrenic," "dangerous" and "not dangerous." We—slave traders and plantation owners, psychiatrists and judges—so label them.

To be sure, some people *are* dangerous. Americans need hardly be reminded of this painful fact. But in American law, dangerousness is not supposed to be an abstract psychological condition attributed to a person; it is supposed to be an inference drawn from the fact that a person has committed a violent act that is illegal, has been charged with it, tried for it, and found guilty of it. In such a case, he should be punished, not treated—in jail, not in a hospital.

II

Admittedly, chattel slavery and psychiatric slavery are not identical, and 1855 is not 1975. Nevertheless, the ideological, economic, political, linguistic, and legal similarities between involuntary servitude and involuntary psychiatry are so commanding that we ignore them at our own peril.

When involuntary servitude flourished, that institution marshaled, and was supported by, the combined forces of popular opinion, science, economic interest (for the dominant classes of society), and, last but not least, legal sanction. Now that involuntary psychiatry flourishes, it commands the support of the same forces. Between the birth of this nation in 1776 and the end of the Civil War in 1865, the courts, including the Supreme Court, repeatedly upheld and strengthened slavery. Psychiatric slavery has been similarly upheld and strengthened by the courts from colonial times to today. Remarking on the legal history of slavery, Leon Higginbotham notes that "[the majority] of the justices of the U.S. Supreme Court from 1789 to 1865 . . . had been slave owners. . . . During the time of slavery, when there were options, the majority of the U.S. Supreme Court chose positions most restrictive to blacks."[2]

The fact that mental patients have fared little better supports the cynical observation that the Supreme Court follows the elections. In the long run and for the sake of the integrity and stability of our form of government, this may be a good rather than a bad thing. In any case, these historical considerations—about both involuntary servitude and involuntary psychiatry—suggest that the remedy for such evils lies not in reforms through the courts but in a change in popular passions, or in legislative leadership, or perhaps in a combination of both.

III

In the meanwhile, psychiatric slavery, although under attack, continues to flourish. In their unanimous opinion in *Donaldson*, the justices declared: "We need not decide whether, when, or by what procedures, a mentally ill person may be confined by the State on any of the grounds which, under contemporary statutes, are generally advanced to justify involuntary confinement of such a person."[3]

The crucial question thus remains unanswered: On what grounds, if any, may an individual be deprived of liberty by being incarcerated in a mental hospital? To appreciate the absurdity and the enormity of the Supreme Court's determination to evade this question but nevertheless rule on the *Donaldson* case, let us pursue further our scrutiny of the parallels between involuntary servitude and involuntary psychiatry.

Suppose that, in a society that accepted and authorized slavery, an ex-slave sued his former master for mistreatment while he was enslaved. How could such a claim be litigated without coming to grips with the issue of slavery? The attempt to do so would be sophistry. Yet, if we substitute involuntary psychiatry for involuntary servitude, that is precisely what all the protagonists in the *Donaldson* case have done.

Donaldson, speaking through his champions, pleads: "Never mind about why I was committed, and by all means never mind what commitment is all about. Just say that I was entitled to a 'treatment' of which I was 'deprived,' and punish the psychiatrists who, as agents of the state, obeyed its courts and implemented its laws." Donaldson thus avoids touching on the sensitive issue of psychiatric slavery, as if he feared that doing so would turn the judges against him.

O'Connor, perhaps realizing that to put up an effective defense he would have to incriminate the whole psychiatric profession as a guild of slave-holders and plantation operators, puts up virtually no defense at all. He could have said: "Let us stop all this nonsense about hospitals and treatment. I never asked for or wanted Donaldson. He was sent to us by his father and the courts. I gave his father and the courts every opportunity to take him back. They never did. What, then, do you want of me?" But to say that would have required that O'Connor admit that his real job was not to cure disease but to control deviance.

The courts, for their part, entered eagerly into this game of deception and self-deception by agreeing to the fundamental rule of psychiatry—namely, that one must never speak in plain English about obvious acts but must always speak in the professional jargon of mad-doctoring about pretended purposes.

Extending the parallels between involuntary servitude and involuntary psychiatry further still, let us assume that, in the hypothetical society which accepts slavery, rules exist for freeing slaves. When, in the master's professional opinion, together perhaps with the opinion of other slaveholders, the slave is idle and can live as a free man, then, under these rules, a master must manumit his slave. Let us assume, further, that a slave, freed under this rule after a bondage of fourteen years, sued his former master for postponing his release unconstitutionally. Absurd as they may seem, these were the contentions the Supreme Court was asked to hear when it was petitioned to hear the *Donaldson* case. Upon them, briefs were written, arguments were heard, and judgment was granted—although the issue of slavery was never raised!

Since the rules governing release from psychiatric slavery clearly specify that the institutional psychiatrist must free those patients who, in his own professional judgment, merit release, legislatures and courts cannot give psychiatrists discretionary powers to release or to retain mental patients, and then try to regulate what is explicitly intended to be a discretionary power. To correct the abuses of the psychiatrist's arbitrary power to confine and release mental hospital patients, the legislatures and the courts have only two alternatives. Either they must limit the psychiatrist's powers to confine and release by assuming more of these powers themselves. This would make it more obvious that the institutional psychiatrist functions as a jailer, that the inmates of his institution are prisoners, and that their relation to each other is governed by the legislatures and the courts. Or they must abolish psychiatric imprisonment, psychiatric prisons, and the whole system of involuntary psychiatry.

This presents the *dramatis personae* of psychiatric slavery with a wonderfully ironic dilemma. At long last, the administrators of psychiatric justice are beginning to realize that they are sitting astride a furious tiger, which they are rightly afraid to dismount. They should never have tried to ride the beast in the first place.

Notes

Preface to the Original Edition (pp. xxiii–xxvi)

1. Weaver, R. M., *Life Without Prejudice, and Other Essays* (Chicago: Regnery, 1965).
2. See Muller, M. J., *O'Connor* v. *Donaldson:* A right to liberty for the nondangerous mentally ill, *Ohio Northern University Law Review*, 3:550–562, 1975, p. 555.

Epigraphs (p. xxix)

1. Davis, D. B., *The Problem of Slavery in Western Culture* (Ithaca, N.Y.: Cornell University Press, 1966), pp. 91–92.
2. *Ibid.,* p. 186.

3. Dumond, D. L., *Antislavery: The Crusade for Freedom* (Ann Arbor, Michigan: University of Michigan Press, 1961), p. 95.

Chapter 1 (pp. 1–12)

1. See, generally, Szasz, T. S., *Law, Liberty, and Psychiatry: An Inquiry into the Social Uses of Mental Health Practices* (New York: Macmillan, 1963), and *Psychiatric Justice* (New York: Macmillan, 1965).

2. See, for example, *Durham* v. *United States*, 214 F 2d, 862 (D.C. Circ., 1954).

3. In this connection, see Szasz, T. S., *The Second Sin* (Garden City, N.Y.: Doubleday Anchor, 1973), and *Heresies* (Garden City, N.Y.: Doubleday Anchor, 1976).

4. Moore, M. S., Some myths about "mental illness," *Archives of General Psychiatry*, 32:1483–1497 (Dec.), 1975, p. 1496.

5. See Szasz, T. S., *The Manufacture of Madness: A Comparative Study of the Inquisition and the Mental Health Movement* (New York: Harper & Row, 1970).

6. See Szasz, T. S., The ACLU's "mental illness" cop-out, *Reason*, 5:4–9 (Jan.), 1974.

7. See Szasz, T. S., The danger of coercive psychiatry, *American Bar Association Journal*, 61:1246–1248 (Oct.), 1975.

Chapter 2 (pp. 13–33)

1. Ennis, B., *Prisoners of Psychiatry: Mental Patients, Psychiatrists, and the Law* (New York: Harcourt, Brace, Jovanovich, 1972), p. 84.

2. See Szasz, T. S., *The Myth of Mental Illness*, revised ed., (New York: Harper & Row, 1974) and *Schizophrenia: The Sacred Symbol of Psychiatry* (New York: Basic Books, 1976).

3. Ennis, *op. cit.*, p. 87.

4. Pear, R., Vindication at last: A patient refused to admit illness, *Washington Star*, June 27, 1975, p. 1.

5. Donaldson, K., *Insanity Inside Out* (New York: Crown, 1976), p. 15.

6. *Ibid.*, pp. 26–27.

7. *Ibid.*, p. 26.

8. *Ibid.*

9. Pear, R., Vindication at last, *op. cit.*

10. Donaldson, K., Blazing a trail for mental patients who want to get out: Kenneth Donaldson tells his own story, *Harper's Weekly*, 63:3 (July 25), 1975.

11. *Ibid.*

12. *Donaldson v. O'Connor*, 493 F 2d, 507 (1974), p. 510.

13. *Ibid.*

14. See, for example, Kolb, L. C., *Noyes' Modern Clinical Psychiatry*, seventh ed. (Philadelphia: Saunders, 1968), pp. 380–382.

15. *Donaldson v. O'Connor*, op. cit., p. 511.

16. Refusal of treatment upheld, *American Medical News*, June 12, 1971, p. 14.

17. *Donaldson v. O'Connor*, *op. cit.*, p. 511.

18. Patient No. A-25738 (Donaldson, K.), Right to treatment inside out, *Georgetown Law Journal* 57:194–198 (March), 1969, p. 194.

19. *O'Connor v. Donaldson*, 422 U.S. 563 (1975), p. 572.

20. *Ibid.*, p. 570.

21. Donaldson, K., *Georgetown Law Journal*, *op. cit.*, p. 196.

22. Birnbaum, M., The Right to Treatment: Some Comments on Its Development, in Ayd, F. J., ed., *Medical, Moral, and Legal Issues in Mental Health Care*, pp. 97–141 (Baltimore: Williams & Wilkins, 1974), p. 117.

23. In this connection, see Szasz, T. S., *Schizophrenia: The Sacred Symbol of Psychiatry* (New York: Basic Books, 1976), especially Chapter 4.

24. Donaldson, K., *Insanity Inside Out*, op. cit., p. 283.

25. *Ibid.*, p. 231.

26. *Ibid.*, pp. 231–234.

27. Birnbaum, M., The Right to Treatment, *op. cit.*, p. 117.
28. Ennis, B., *Prisoners of Psychiatry, op. cit.*, pp. 90–92.
29. *Ibid.*, p. 92.
30. *Donaldson v. O'Connor, op. cit.*, p. 523.
31. *Ibid.*, p. 518.
32. *Ibid.*
33. Donaldson, K., *Insanity Inside Out, op. cit.*, p. 318.
34. *Donaldson v. O'Connor, op cit.*, p. 509.
35. *Ibid.*, p. 510.
36. *Ibid.*, p. 511.
37. *Rouse v. Cameron*, 373 F.2d, 451 (1966).
38. *Ibid.*, p. 462.
39. See, generally, Szasz, T. S., *Ideology and Insanity: Essays on the Psychiatric Dehumanization of Man* (Garden City, N.Y.: Doubleday Anchor, 1970); *The Second Sin* (Garden City, N.Y.: Doubleday Anchor, 1973); and *Heresies* (Garden City, N.Y.: Doubleday Anchor, 1976).

Chapter 3 (pp. 34–58)

1. *The Mental Health Law Project, Summary of Activities,* September, 1975, p. 2.
2. See Szasz, T. S., *The Second Sin* (Garden City, N.Y.: Doubleday, 1973), and *Heresies* (Garden City, N.Y.: Doubleday, 1976).
3. Friedman, P. R., Beyond Dixon: The principle of the least restrictive alternative, *The Mental Health Law Project: Summary of Activities,* 2:1 and 3–4 (March), 1976, pp. 3–4.
4. Klein, J. I., Mental health law: Legal doctrine at the crossroads, *ibid.*, pp. 7–10; p. 8.
5. *Ibid.*
6. *Ibid.*
7. *Ibid.*
8. *Ibid.*

9. Quoted in Ridenour, N., *Mental Health in the United States: A Fifty-Year History* (Cambridge: Harvard University Press, 1961), p. 39.

10. See Szasz, *Ideology and Insanity* (Garden City, N.Y.: Doubleday Anchor, 1970), especially p. 220.

11. Zilboorg, G., Misconceptions of legal insanity, *American Journal of Orthopsychiatry*, 9:540–553 (July), 1939, p. 550.

12. See, Arens, R., *Make Mad the Guilty: The Insanity Defense in the District of Columbia* (Springfield, Ill.: Charles C Thomas, 1969).

13. Markmann, C. L., *The Noblest Cry: A History of the American Civil Liberties Union* (New York: St. Martin's Press, 1965), pp. 400–401.

14. See Szasz, T. S., The ACLU's "mental illness" cop-out, *Reason*, 5:4–9 (Jan.), 1974.

15. See Bazelon, D., The law and the mentally ill, *American Journal of Psychiatry*, 125:665–669 (Nov.), 1968, p. 667.

16. Clark, R., *Crime in America: Observations on its Nature, Causes, Prevention, and Control* (New York: Simon and Shuster, 1970), pp. 75–76.

17. The first landmark: Mental patients' rights, *Civil Liberties*, September 1972, p. 5.

18. Donaldson, K., *Insanity Inside Out* (New York: Crown, 1976), p. 361.

19. *O'Connor* v. *Donaldson*, Brief for the Respondent, Mimeographed, 1974, p. 31.

20. *Ibid.*

21. *Jackson* v. *Indiana*, 406 U.S. 715 (1972), pp. 737–738; cited in Brief for the Respondent, p. 33.

22. Schwartz, B. M., In the name of treatment: Autonomy, civil commitment, and right to refuse treatment, *Notre Dame Lawyer*, 50:808–842 (June), 1975, p. 808.

23. *O'Connor* v. *Donaldson*, Brief for Respondent, *op. cit.*, pp. 34–36.

24. See, Official actions, Amicus curiae brief in the Donaldson

case, *American Journal of Psychiatry*, 132:109–115 (Jan.), 1975; APA enters Florida case to defend psychiatrists, *Psychiatric News*, 9:1 and 9 (Oct. 16), 1974; APA sides with psychiatrists in appeal of Donaldson case, *ibid.*, 10:20 (Feb. 5), 1975.

25. Quoted in Ridenour, *op. cit.*, p. 76.

26. Council of the American Psychiatric Association, Position statement on the question of adequacy of treatment, *American Journal of Psychiatry*, 123:1458–1460 (May), 1967, p. 1459.

27. *Ibid.*, p. 1458.

28. Schwartz, B. M., In the name of treatment, *op. cit.*, p. 809.

29. See Szasz, T. S., *Law, Liberty, and Psychiatry: An Inquiry into the Social Uses of Mental Health Practices* (New York: Macmillan, 1963), pp. 199–211.

30. See Szasz, T. S., *Psychiatric Justice* (New York: Macmillan, 1965), pp. 178–225.

31. See, for example, Lang, J. S., Some White House visitors sent to mental ward, *The News and Observer* (Raleigh, N.C.), Apr. 26, 1971, p. 2; and White House visits end in nut house, *Atlantic City Press*, Apr. 26, 1971, p. 14.

32. Cited in, U.S. backs treatment as a right of mental patients, *The New York Times*, Jan. 16, 1975, p. 10.

33. Cited in, Constitutional rights vanish: Elderly, poor denied free choice of doctor, *AAPS* [American Association of Physicians and Surgeons] *Newsletter*, 29:1–2 (Nov.), 1975, p. 1.

34. See, generally, Chapter 8 herein.

35. *O'Connor* v. *Donaldson*, Brief for the Respondent, *op. cit.*, p. 38.

36. See pp. 5–7.

37. *O'Connor* v. *Donaldson*, Brief for the Respondent, *op. cit.*, p. 42.

38. Donaldson, K., *Insanity Inside Out* (New York: Crown, 1976), p. 69.

39. *Ibid.*, pp. 68–69.

40. Kesey, K., *One Flew Over the Cuckoo's Nest* (New York: Viking, 1962).

41. *O'Connor* v. *Donaldson,* Brief for the Respondent, *op. cit.*, p. 53.

42. See, for example, Szasz, T. S., ed., *The Age of Madness: A History of Involuntary Mental Hospitalization Presented in Selected Texts* (Garden City, N.Y.: Doubleday Anchor, 1973).

43. MHLP, Bylaws (Mimeographed, 1973), p. 1.

44. MHLP lists priorities, sets goals, *The Mental Health Law Project: Summary of Activities,* June, 1975, p. 11.

45. MHLP, Procedures for voluntary treatment (Mimeographed, 1975), p. 1.

46. *Ibid.*, p. 2.

Chapter 4 (pp. 59–65)

1. *O'Connor* v. *Donaldson,* Brief for the Petitioner, Mimeographed, December 5, 1975, p. 5.

2. See pp. 30, 50, 79–82.

3. See pp. 59–63.

4. *O'Connor* v. *Donaldson, op. cit.*, p. 5.

5. *Ibid.*

6. *Ibid.*, pp. 8–9.

7. *Ibid.*, p. 9.

8. *Ibid.*, pp. 9–10.

9. See Szasz, T. S., *Schizophrenia: The Sacred Symbol of Psychiatry* (New York: Basic Books, 1976), especially pp. 153–167.

10. *O'Connor* v. *Donaldson, op. cit., p.* 10.

11. *Ibid.*, p. 31.

12. *Ibid.*, p. 50.

13. *Ibid.*, pp. 55–56.

Chapter 5 (pp. 66–75)

1. Stone, A. A., in Official actions: *Amicus curiae* brief in the Donaldson case, *American Journal of Psychiatry,* 132:109–115 (Jan.), 1975, p. 109.

2. *O'Connor* v. *Donaldson,* 422 U.S. 563 (1975), p. 576.

3. APA enters Florida case to defend psychiatrists, *Psychiatric News,* 9:1 and 9, (Oct. 16), 1974; see also the followup story, APA sides with psychiatrists in appeal of Donaldson case, *ibid.,* 10:20 (Feb. 5), 1975.

4. *Ibid.*

5. Stone, A. A., Official actions, *ibid.*

6. See Szasz, T. S., *Law, Liberty, and Psychiatry: An Inquiry into the Social Uses of Mental Health Practices* (New York: Macmillan, 1973), especially pp. 39–71.

7. Official actions, *op. cit.,* p. 111.

8. *O'Connor* v. *Donaldson, op. cit.,* p. 576.

9. Official actions, *op. cit.,* p. 111.

10. See Chapter 8 herein.

11. Official actions, *op. cit.,* p. 114.

12. *Ibid.,* p. 111.

13. *Ibid.*

14. *Ibid.*

15. *Ibid.*

16. *Ibid.,* p. 114.

17. Rush, B., Observations intended to favour a supposition that black Color (as it is called) of the Negroes is derived from the LEPROSY, *Transactions of the American Philosophical Society,* 4: 289–297, 1799; in this connection, see Szasz, T. S., *The Manufacture of Madness: A Comparative Study of the Inquisition and the Mental Health Movement.* (New York: Harper & Row, 1970) pp. 153–159.

18. Cartwright, S. A., Report of the diseases and physical peculiarities of the negro race, *New Orleans Medical and*

Surgical Journal, 7:691–715, 1851; in this connection, see Szasz, T. S. The sane slave: An historical note on the use of medical diagnosis as justificatory rhetoric, *American Journal of Psychotherapy,* 25:228–239 (Apr.), 1971.

19. Official actions, *op. cit.,* p. 114.

Chapter 6 (pp. 76–88)

1. *O'Connor* v. *Donaldson,* 422 U.S. 563 (1975), p. 563.

2. *Ibid.*

3. *Ibid.,* pp. 572–573.

4. See pp. 32–33; also Szasz, T. S., *Law, Liberty and Psychiatry: An Inquiry Into the Social Uses of Mental Health Practices* (New York: Macmillan, 1963), and The right to health, *Georgetown Law Journal,* 57:734–751 (March), 1969.

5. *O'Connor* v. *Donaldson, op. cit.,* p. 573.

6. *Ibid.,* pp. 573–574.

7. *Ibid.,* p. 576.

8. *Ibid.,* p. 577.

9. See, for example, Cover, R. M., *Justice Accused: Antislavery and the Judicial Process* (New Haven: Yale University Press, 1975).

10. *O'Connor* v. *Donaldson, op. cit.,* p. 577.

11. *Ibid.*

12. Kopolow, L. E., A review of major implications of the *O'Connor* v. *Donaldson* decision, *American Journal of Psychiatry,* 133:379–383 (Apr.), 1976, p. 380.

13. Muller, M. J., *O'Connor* v. *Donaldson:* A right to liberty for the nondangerous mentally ill. *Ohio Northern University Law Review,* 3:550–562, 1975, p. 550.

14. See Szasz, T. S., Involuntary Mental Hospitalization: A Crime Against Humanity, in *Ideology and Insanity: Essays on the Psychiatric Dehumanization of Man,* pp. 113–139 (Garden City, NY: Doubleday Anchor, 1970).

15. *O'Connor* v. *Donaldson, op. cit.,* p. 579.

16. *Ibid.*
17. *Ibid.*, pp. 582–583.
18. *Ibid.*, pp.583–584.
19. *Ibid.*, pp. 579–580.
20. *Ibid.*, pp. 587–589.

Chapter 7 (pp. 89–108)

1. MacKenzie, J. P. and Greider, W., Historic mental health ruling, *The Washington Post,* June 27, 1975, pp. A1 and A6.
2. *Ibid.*, p. A1.
3. *Ibid.*, p. A6.
4. Weaver, W., Jr., High court curbs power to confine the mentally ill, *The New York Times,* June 27, 1975, pp. 1 and 30.
5. *Ibid.*, p. 30.
6. *Ibid.*
7. Brown, B. S., Introduction, in National Institute of Mental Health, *Memo from the Director,* December 1975, p. 7.
8. Opening the asylums, *Time,* July 7, 1975, p. 44.
9. *Ibid.*
10. *Ibid.*
11. Freeing mental patients, *Newsweek,* July 7, 1975, p. 45
12. Cited in MacKenzie and Greider, *op. cit.,* p. A6.
13. Freeing mental patients, *op. cit.*
14. High court upholds Donaldson, *Civil Liberties,* Sept. 1975, pp. 1 & 7.
15. *Ibid.*, p. 1.
16. *Ibid.*
17. See pp. 41–43.
18. Donaldson, K., *Insanity Inside Out* (New York: Crown, 1976), see especially pp. 283–284.
19. Birnbaum, M., The Right to Treatment: Some Comments on Its Development, in Ayd, F. J., ed., *Medical, Moral,*

and Legal Issues in Mental Health Care, pp. 97–141 (Baltimore: Williams & Wilkins, 1974), p. 111.

20. Friedman, P. R., The Supreme Court unlocks doors, *Mental Health Law Project: Summary of Activities,* Sept., 1975, pp. 11–12; p. 11.

21. *Ibid.*

22. *Ibid.*

23. Court rulings moving to insure right to treatment for hospitalized mental patients, *American Medical News,* Oct. 6, 1975, p. 9.

24. Whose right to what treatment and who foots the bill? *Roche Report: Frontiers of Psychiatry,* 5:1–2 (Oct. 1), 1975; p. 1.

25. 'Right to liberty' ruling raises major questions, *Clinical Psychiatry News,* July 1975, pp. 1 and 30–31; p. 30.

26. *Ibid.*

27. *Ibid.,* p. 31.

28. *Ibid.*

29. *Emery* v. *State,* 483 P 2d, 1296 (1971).

30. See Szasz, T. S., Voluntary mental hospitalization: An unacknowledged practice of medical fraud, *New England Journal of Medicine,* 287:277–278 (Aug. 10), 1972.

31. Cited in 'Right to liberty' ruling raises major questions, *op. cit.,* p. 31.

32. Overholser, W., Statement, in *Constitutional Rights of the Mentally Ill* (Washington, D. C.: U.S. Government Printing Office, 1961), pp. 19–40; p. 21.

33. Donaldson decision seen having minimal effects on hospitals, *Clinical Psychiatry News,* Aug., 1975, pp. 1 and 22.

34. *Ibid.,* pp. 1 and 22.

35. Ruling on mental patients' rights debated, *Medical Tribune,* Aug. 20, 1975, p. 2.

36. *Ibid.*

37. Quoted in, McDonald, M., Supreme Court rules on *Don-*

aldson v. *O'Connor, Psychiatric News,* 10:1 and 22–23 (July 16), 1975; p. 23.

38. Rensberger, B., Ruling on confining mentally ill argued, *The New York Times,* Aug. 17, 1975, pp. 1 and 24; p. 1.

39. *Ibid.*

40. *Ibid.,* p. 24.

41. *Ibid.*

42. Stanton, R., Involuntary civil commitment proceedings: Some further thoughts, *New Jersey Law Journal,* 98:1 & 10–11 (Sept. 11), 1975, p. 1.

43. *Ibid.,* p. 10.

44. *Ibid.,* p. 11.

45. Muller, M. J., *O'Connor* v. *Donaldson:* A right to liberty for the nondangerous mentally ill, *Ohio Northern University Law Review,* 3:550–562, 1975; p. 550.

46. Wealthy beggar ordered committed, *The News-Sun* (Waukegan, Ill.), Aug. 4, 1975, p. 50.

47. *Ibid.*

48. *Ibid.*

49. See Szasz, T. S., *Law, Liberty, and Psychiatry: An Inquiry into the Social Uses of Mental Health Practices* New York: Macmillan, 1963), pp. 215–216.

50. See, for example, Szasz, T. S., ed., *The Age of Madness: A History of Involuntary Mental Hospitalization Presented in Selected Texts* (Garden City, N. Y.: Doubleday Anchor, 1973), especially pp. 5–17, 53–81, and 127–150.

Chapter 8 (pp. 109–132)

1. See, for example, Hunter, R. and MacAlpine, I., *Three Hundred Years of Psychiatry, 1535–1860* (London: Oxford University Press, 1963); Szasz, T. S., ed., *The Age of Madness: A History of Involuntary Mental Hospitalization Presented in Selected Texts* (Garden City, N. Y., Doubleday Anchor, 1973); and Skultans, V., *Madness and*

Morals: Ideas of Insanity in the Nineteenth Century (London: Routledge, 1975).

2. See Szasz, T. S., *The Ethics of Psychoanalysis: The Theory and Method of Autonomous Psychotherapy* (New York: Basic Books, 1965).

3. Jaspers, K., *General Psychopathology* [1923], trans. by J. Hoenig and M. W. Hamilton (Chicago: University of Chicago Press, 1963), pp. 839–840.

4. See Szasz, T. S., The right to health, *Georgetown Law Journal*, 57:734–751 (March), 1969.

5. *West Virginia Board of Education* v. *Barnette*, 319 U.S. 624 (1943), p. 633.

6. *Ibid.*, p. 642.

7. See, generally, Szasz, T. S., *The Manufacture of Madness: A Comparative Study of the Inquisition and the Mental Health Movement* (New York: Harper & Row, 1970).

8. Rush, B., Letter to Granville Sharp, November 28, 1783, *Journal of American Studies*, 1:1–32 (April 1), 1967, p. 20.

9. See Szasz, *The Manufacture of Madness, op. cit.*, pp. 151–153.

10. Quoted in Binger, C., *Revolutionary Doctor: Benjamin Rush, 1746–1813* (New York: Norton, 1966), p. 288.

11. Rush, B., *Medical Inquiries and Observations Upon the Diseases of the Mind [1812]* (New York: Hafner, 1962), p. 339.

12. Ray, I., *A Treatise on the Medical Jurisprudence of Insanity* [1838] (Cambridge, Mass.: Harvard University Press, 1962), p. 339.

13. Alexander, F., and Staub, H., *The Criminal, the Judge, and the Public: A Psychological Analysis* [1929], revised ed. (Glencoe, Ill.: The Free Press, 1956), p. xiii.

14. Menninger, K., *The Crime of Punishment* (New York: Knopf 1968), p. 17.

15. Arens, R., *Make Mad the Guilty: The Insanity Defense in the District of Columbia* (Springfield, Ill.: Charles C Thomas, 1969).

16. Bazelon, D., The awesome decision, *The Saturday Evening Post*, Jan. 23, 1960, pp. 33 and 53–56; p. 56.
17. Bazelon, D., Justice stumbles over science, *Trans-action*, 4:8–17 (July-Aug.), 1967, p. 13.
18. Bazelon, D., The law and the mentally ill, *American Journal of Psychiatry*, 125:665–669 (Nov.), 1968, p. 667.
19. Kolb, L. C., *Noyes' Modern Clinical Psychiatry*, seventh ed. (Philadelphia: Saunders, 1968), p. 513.
20. *Ibid.*, p. 514.
21. Stone, A. A., Overview: The right to treatment—Comments on the law and its impact, *American Journal of Psychiatry*, 132:1125–1134 (Nov.), 1975.
22. *Ibid., p.* 1126.
23. *Ibid.*
24. *Ibid.*
25. In this connection, see Szasz, T. S., *Psychiatric Justice* (New York: Macmillan, 1965).
26. *Donaldson* v. *O'Connor*, 493 F. 2d 507 (5th Cir. 1974), p. 508.
27. Stone, An overview, *op. cit.*, p. 1130.
28. *Ibid.*, p. 1131.
29. *Ibid.*, pp. 1129, 1133.
30. Contemporary Literature, Report of the proceedings of the Association of Medical Superintendents of American Institutions for the Insane, at their twenty-second annual meeting, Boston, June 2–5, 1868, in Hammond, W. A., ed., *The Quarterly Journal of Psychological Medicine and Jurisprudence*, Vol. II, pp. 495–505 (New York: D. Appleton and Company, 1869), p. 495.
31. Birnbaum, M., The right to treatment, *American Bar Association Journal*, 46:499–502 (May) 1960, p. 499.
32. Szasz, T. S., *Law, Liberty, and Psychiatry: An Inquiry into the Social Uses of Mental Health Practices* (New York: Macmillan, 1963), pp. 214–215.
33. Birnbaum, M., The Right to Treatment: Some Comments on Its Development, in Ayd, F. J., ed., *Medical, Moral,*

153

and Legal Issues in Mental Health Care, pp. 97–141 (Baltimore: Williams & Wilkins, 1974), p. 128.

34. *Ibid.,* p. 129.

35. *Ibid.,* pp. 130–131.

36. *Ibid.,* p. 134.

37. Rensberger, B., New suit presses "right to treatment" for mentally ill, *The New York Times,* Sept. 25, 1975, p. 26.

38. Quoted in Herndon, A., New right-to-treatment suit filed in New York, *Psychiatric News,* 10:1, 27 & 35 (Nov. 5), 1975, p. 27.

Chapter 9 (pp. 133–139)

1. *O'Connor v. Donaldson,* 422 U.S. 563 (1975).

2. Higginbotham, A. L., Jr., Racism and the early American legal process, 1619–1896, *Annals of the American Academy of Political and Social Science,* 407:1–17 (May), 1973, pp. 11–12.

3. *O'Connor v. Donaldson, op. cit.,* p. 573.

Index

Adair, Clark, 60
Alexander, Franz, 112, 114, 119
American Association of Mental
   Deficiency, xn
American Association of Physicians
   and Surgeons (AAPS), 49n,
   50n
American Bar Association Journal,
   125
American Civil Liberties Union
   (ACLU), 8, 28, 36, 54, 55,
   93–94, 105, 115
   psychiatric positions, 41–43, 55
American Federation of State,
   County and Municipal
   Employees A.F.L.–C.I.O., xn
American Medical News, 95

American Orthopsychiatric
   Association (AOA), xn, 36,
   43, 117
   psychiatric positions, 40–41
American Psychiatric Association
   (APA), xn, 47, 105, 117
   Donaldson brief, 66–75
American Psychological
   Association, xn
Arens, Richard, 116n
Association of Medical
   Superintendents of American
   Institutions for the Insane,
   47–48, 125n

Bazelon, David, 31, 41, 105, 111,
   112

Benbow, J. T., 52n
Birnbaum, Morton, 25, 26, 42–43,
    93, 94n, 98–99, 105, 111,
    125–132
Bork, Robert H., 49n, 50n
Brooklyn State Hospital, 128, 129
Brown, Bertram S., 90, 92n, 97
Burger, Warren E., 84–88, 95, 124

Calhoun, Franklin J., 62
Cartwright, Samuel, 74
Center for Law and Social Policy,
    36
Christian Science, 22–25, 58
Christmas, June Jackson, 36
Civil Liberties, 93
Clark, Ramsey, 41–42
Clinical Psychiatry News, 96–98
Coerced psychiatric personality
    change, 111
Commitment, 13–21, 30, 32–33,
    41–42, 46–47, 50, 53, 60,
    78, 101–103
Constitution of the United States,
    5
Curability, cult of, 112

Danaher, John A., 31n, 32n
Dangerousness, 44–45, 60–63,
    80–82, 135
Dix, Dorothea, 43, 112
Donaldson, Kenneth
    American Civil Liberties Union
        and, 28
    American Psychiatric
        Association brief, 66–75
    autobiography, 18, 42, 52n, 93n
    Burger's opinion in *O'Connor v.
        Donaldson*, 84–88
    class action suit, 28–29
    commitment to Florida State
        Hospital, 13–21, 30, 46, 60
    dangerousness issue, 44–45,
        60–63, 80–82, 135
    discharge from Florida State
        Hospital, 26–29

Donaldson v. O'Connor, 22, 23,
    29–31, 83, 122
    interpretations of *O'Connor v.
        Donaldson*, 89–108
    in Marcy State Hospital, 15, 18
    Mental Health Law Project and,
        20–21, 34–35
    Mental Health Law Project
        brief, 44–48, 50–53, 57–58,
        62
    O'Connor brief, 59–65
    paranoid schizophrenic,
        diagnosed as, 22, 44, 60–63
    religion of, 22–25, 58, 83
    in Syracuse Psychopathic
        Hospital, 18, 19
Donaldson, Marjorie K., 52n
Donaldson, Olive J., 18, 19
Donaldson, William T., 13–16, 21,
    32, 52n
Donaldson case: *see O'Connor v.
    Donaldson* (1975)
Donaldson v. O'Connor (1974),
    22, 23, 29–31, 83, 122
Downstate Medical Center,
    Brooklyn, 128, 129
Durham rule, 116–117

Electroshock treatment, 22, 24,
    37, 51, 52n
Ennis, Bruce, 14, 15, 16, 20, 25,
    91, 92–93, 111
Explanation, distinction between
    justification and, 1–4

Fifth Circuit Court of Appeals, 31,
    70, 71, 76, 77, 80, 83, 87, 96,
    122
First Amendment, 111
Florida State Hospital,
    Chattahoochee, 13–21, 26–29,
    30, 46, 51, 52n, 72, 73
Ford Foundation, 36, 37
Fourteenth Amendment, 31, 95
Fox, Walter, 51
Friedman, Paul R., 36, 37, 94, 95

156

Index

Friedman, Robert, 104–106
Frontiers of Psychiatry, 95–96
Fugitive slave laws, 131

Genesen, Lawrence L., 104, 106
Georgetown Symposium on the
    Right to Treatment, 24
Group for the Advancement of
    Psychiatry (GAP), 119–120
Gumanis, John, 23, 24, 25, 30, 59,
    116

Habeas corpus, 26, 29, 98–99
Higginbotham, Leon, 136

Involuntary mental hospitalization,
    see Commitment
Involuntary servitude, *see* Slavery

Jackson v. Indiana (1972), 45
Japanese-American relocation
    camps, 55
Jaspers, Karl, 110n
Jefferson, Thomas, 113
Jehovah's Witnesses, 111
Joseph P. Kennedy Foundation, xn
Justification
    distinction between explanation
        and, 1–4
    of human actions, 5–9
    by silence, 5–6

Kesey, Ken, 52n
Klein, Joel, 38, 39
Kolb, Lawrence C., 118–120
Kopolow, Louis, 81–82

Law, Liberty and Psychiatry
    (Szasz), 125

Make Mad the Guilty (Arens),
    116n
Marcy State Hospital, Utica, New
    York, 15, 18, 20
Markmann, Charles, 41
Marmor, Judd, 97
Medicaid, 126

*Medical Inquiries and
    Observations upon the
    Diseases of the Mind* (Rush),
    113
Medical Tribune, 98
Medicare, 126
Menninger, Karl, 40, 41, 112, 115
Mental Health Law Project
    (MHLP), 18, 105, 117, 132
    bylaws, 55–56
    definition of, 35
    Donaldson and, 20–21, 34–35
    Donaldson brief, 44–48, 50–53,
        57–58, 62
    establishment of, 36
    interpretation of *O'Connor v.
        Donaldson*, 94–95
    "Procedures for Voluntary
        Treatment," 57
    psychiatric positions of, 36–40
Mental hospitalization, involuntary,
    see Commitment
Moore, M. S., 7n

National Association for Autistic
    Children, xn
National Association for Mental
    Health, xn
National Association for Retarded
    Citizens, xn
National Center for Law and the
    Handicapped, xn
National health insurance, 120,
    124
National Institute of Mental
    Health (NIMH), 91n, 92n
New Jersey Law Journal, 101
New York Civil Liberties Union,
    91
New York Times, The, 90–91, 99,
    127
Newsweek, 92
Noyes' Modern Clinical Psychiatry
    (Kolb), 118–120

O'Connor, J. B., 24, 25, 27, 44–45,
    52, 116

157

Index

O'Connor, J. B. (*cont.*)
brief for, 59–65
Donaldson v. O'Connor, 22, 23, 29–31, 83, 122
O'Connor v. Donaldson, 34, 76–108, 137–138
O'Connor v. Donaldson (1975), 34, 76–83, 133, 134, 136–138
American Psychiatric Association brief, 66–75
Burger's opinion, 84–88
interpretations of, 89–108
Mental Health Law Project brief, 44–48, 50–53, 57–58, 62
O'Connor brief, 59–65
One Flew Over the Cuckoo's Nest (Kesey), 52n
Overholser, Winfred, 98n

Paranoid schizophrenia, 22, 44–45, 60–63
Parens patriae, doctrine of, 85–86, 104, 105, 127
"Position Statement on the Question of Adequacy of Treatment" (APA), 47–48
Post-commitment rights, 78–79, 83, 96, 103–104
Pound, Ezra, 49
Professional Standards Review Organizations (PSROs), 49n, 50n
Psychiatric News, 67, 99
"Psychiatrically Deviated Sex Offenders" (GAP), 119

Rationality, 7n
Ray, Isaac, 112, 113–114
Red Cross, 54
Religion, freedom of, 111
Rensberger, Boyce, 99–101
Rescue Mission, 54
Responsibility, 116
Right to treatment, *see* Treatment, right to
Rouse v. Cameron (1966), 31, 32n, 121

Rush, Benjamin, 74, 112–113

Salvation Army, 54
Sanism, 127
Saturday Evening Post, 20
Schwartz, Brian, 46, 49n
Self-incrimination, right against, 123
Senate Subcommittee on the Constitutional Rights of the Mentally Ill, 98n
Silence, justification by, 5–6
Slavery, 5, 54, 74, 130–131, 133–136, 138
Soviet Union, psychiatry in, 42n, 117–118
Stanton, Reginald, 101–103
State University of New York, 129
Stewart, Potter, 96
Stone, Alan A., 66–67, 68, 96–97, 120–121, 123–124
Supreme Court of the United States, *see O'Connor v. Donaldson* (1975)
Syracuse Psychopathic Hospital, 18, 19

Termination of care, right to, 56, 57
Thirteenth Amendment, 5n
Time, 92
Tort litigation, 48
Treatment, right to, 22–25, 28, 31, 43, 45, 46–53, 56, 58, 61, 64, 70, 77, 78, 87, 89, 93, 95, 98–99, 105, 109–132

United Nations Human Rights Council, 127
United States Mission on Mental Health, 117
Utah Supreme Court, 97

Visotsky, Harold, 36
Voluntary mental hospitalization, 57, 97

Index

Walker, Edwin, 49
Washington Post, 90, 92
Washington Star, 17, 19
Weaver, Richard, ix
Weinberger, Caspar, 128

Wisdom, John Minor, 22, 23, 31
Woe v. Weinberger (1975),
128–131

Zilboorg, Gregory, 40

159